To, GRAHAM

LOVE FROM
JANE, CLIVE
NICOLA & ZOE

JUNE 97.

To Robert Bassett

Published by Corridor Press,
21 South Street,
Reading RG1 4QR

Telephone 01734 391029

Printed in Great Britain by Lamport Gilbert Limited,
117 Wantage Road, Reading, Berkshire RG30 2SW, England.

ISBN NUMBER 1 897715 10 2

Moments *of* Glory

the story of football in Reading

CORRIDOR

PRESS

Preface

The idea for a book on local football came about long before Reading FC's dramatic progess to the Wembley play-off last year, but the reaction throughout the town, that surge of interest and enthusiasm and the sense of local pride, confirmed our feeling that Moments of Glory would be a good community project. The love of football is a great unifier and Reading, as many of our contributors have pointed out, has always been a football crazy town.

For a community publisher like Corridor Press, football fulfils all its aims – it goes right across the board, transcending age, race, religion, class and gender. It also embraces all levels of skills, which is why we have written about the whole range of local football – street and school, park and professional.

We produce our books through the hard work and enthusiasm of volunteers who follow the project through from idea to publication. They make all the decisions about the book – its contents, design, title and price – and the amount of time they put into the project can be anything from a few hours to a longer-term commitment to Corridor Press. As the book goes into production, dozens more contributors are drawn in. Some write or tell their stories, carry out research, take photographs, help to lay out and design the book, and then market and sell it.

During this process we run workshops for people who work on the book or are involved in their own book projects. More than 100 people have been involved, in a variety of ways, in the production of Moments of Glory, a project which was started in May 1995 and culminated in the publication of the book nine months later.

Corridor Press is a non-profit organisation and special thanks are due to our funders Southern Arts, Reading Borough Council and Berks County Council, who are responsible for our existence. We are also grateful to the Reading Evening Post, which always gives our projects tremendous support, and the Paul Hamlyn Foundation, which generously funds our training programme.

Thanks, too, to Imogen and Damian Clarke, of Imaging Design, for their unfailing support, both professional and personal, and to all the regular volunteers who have given us hours of their time so willingly.

We are also grateful to Adrian Porter, of Reading FC, for his support, to all those involved in the local football scene who have given us their time, knowledge and enthusiasm, and to those who have subscribed to the book.

■ Corridor Press runs a regular programme throughout the year of workshops on writing, publishing, design and layout, and selling and marketing books. If you want to become involved in forthcoming projects, contact us at Corridor Press, 21 South Street, Reading RG1 4QR, or call (01734) 3910290.

Contents

CONTRIBUTORS

Moments of Glory team
Clive Baskerville
Simon Blackburn
Ben Busfield
Rose Cam
Anne-Marie Dodson
David Downs
Juliet Evans
Mike Facherty
Matthew Farrell
Alison Haymonds
Nicola Hodgson
Bryan Horsnell
Mark Huxtable
Natasha Jordan
Duncan Mitchell
Tim Redgrove
Jayn Ritchie

Production
Linda Barlow
Ben Busfield
Damian Clarke
Imogen Clarke
Anne-Marie Dodson
Jean Duval
Shane Edwards
Mike Facherty
Matthew Farrell
Alison Haymonds
Nicola Hodgson
Mark Huxtable
Natasha Jordan
Linda Maestranzi
Stuart Mills
Beryl Pearson
Manjinder Sidhu

Photographs, cartoons and illustrations
Areff (Ron Fennell)

Jonnie Blackburn
Thomas Clapham
Daniel Earwicker
C S (Snooper) Jones
Syd Jordan
Bryan McAllister
Reading Evening Post
Tim Redgrove
Hilton Tims

Contributors
Peter Adams
Marilyn Ballard
Daniel Bamford
Terry Bampton
Tony Bampton
David Barr
Peter Bartlett
Clive Baskerville
Annie Bassett
Peter Baxter
Bob Bennett
Joan Bennett
Trish Bennett
Simon Blackburn
Andrew Brown
Roy Budd
Bill Cam
Elsie Chalker
Alison Chapman
Lisa Collins
Doug Cunningham
Paddy Davis
John Dell
Rachel Dowling
David Downs
Paul Dunn
Patrick Dunne
Ed Edwards
Barry Elmore

Donna Eustace
Matthew Facherty
Wilf Fewtrell
Roland Ford
Mike Foster
Debbie Fry
Peter Glanville
Frank Glasspool
Alan Glenny
Ian Godfrey
Stuart Godfrey
Len Grant
Stephen Green
Ann Grosfort
Norrie Hart
Linda Hicks
Petra Hill
Terri Hinton
Cathy Holwill
Bryan Horsnell
Chris Huntley
Jack Ingram
Jack Jarvis
David Jeanes
Richard Johnson
Jimmy Jones
Philip Lewis
Simon Lovell
Stuart Lovell
Johnny Mapson
George Marks
Sam Maynard
Joe McGough
Gerry McGreevy
Betty Millard
Fred Millard
Nick Milne
Duncan Mitchell
Phil Mitchell
John Moore
Roy Murdoch
MC Naptalie
Gordon Neate

Viv Neate
Maurice O'Brien
Roisin O'Callaghan
Keith Orwin
Alan Porton
Mick Price
Gary Purser
John Roper
Barney Rubble
Bob Russell
Rev Peter Smith
Terry Spice
Nigel Sutcliffe
Steve Thomson
Peter Toft
Reesy Trenchard
John Waters
Danny Webb
Neil Webb
Michael Welch
Micky Wells
Emily Wilkinson
Adrian Williams
Andy Winterbottom
Les Withers
Brian Wooldridge

Geoffrey Field Junior School
Ranikhet Junior School
Westwood Farm Junior School

Cover
Damian Clarke
Tim Redgrove

Introduction

Moments of Glory: the story of football in Reading

by Neil Webb

I am pleased to have the opportunity of writing the introduction to a book about football in my home town of Reading, because that is where my formative football years were spent.

I was involved in football as soon as I was born because my father Doug was playing for Reading FC at the time. As soon as I went to Birch Copse Primary School, I played in midfield for the school team, and at the age of nine, was selected to play for the Reading Schools representative team.

At my secondary school, Little Heath in Tilehurst, I was made captain of the school teams from under-12s to under-15s. Sometimes, if I did not have a school game, I would play for the Reading Reserves team in the Football Combination League. I can even remember having to leave a GCE 'O' Level practical exam halfway through because I had to catch the reserve team bus for an away team. My life was full of football, and at weekends I played for two more teams, Caversham Boys and Southcote United, who were in the Reading Sunday Youth League.

When I left school I joined Reading FC as an apprentice, and was lucky enough to make my debut for the first team when I was still only 16. I was also selected for the England Youth side, and my career took me to Portsmouth, Nottingham Forest, Manchester United and the full England International team.

The rest of my family have also been connected with football in Reading. My brother Gary was a more than useful local footballer who played for Peppard; my mother Joan worked in the office at Elm Park for many years; my father Doug became the Reading FC physiotherapist and youth team manager after his playing career ended, and I married Shelley, whose father, Tony Alexander, had also played for Reading in the 1950s.

My interest in local football came full circle at the start of the current season when I watched Reading's game against Derby County from the terraces, the first time I had done so since I was a youngster. You can imagine how the memories came flooding back.

I have so many reasons for being grateful to football in Reading. I enjoyed every game I played, those on the parks and school pitches in Reading as much as those at Wembley. I wish this book every success and I also wish good luck to everyone involved in the sport in Reading.

1 A Good Place to Start

Street and School Football

STREET FOOTBALL

For most people the story of football starts in the simplest way – kicking around with a ball in the street or recreation ground. Reading FC's star player Stuart Lovell was no exception.

'We were lucky living in an area of Caversham Park where there was a large playing area. We spent most of our childhood outside, particularly during the holidays, kicking or hitting a ball around and using the walls in our close as an enclosed court. We made that area into a six-a-side pitch and that's where I gained a lot of my sporting education.

'The other day I was back around that area where I learned to kick the ball up against a wall, and decided to try it once more for old times' sake. But when I got out there I noticed a sign that said "Ball games strictly prohibited". As I wandered about with a ball in my hand, a chap came out and shouted at me that he'd call the police if I started kicking it around.

'I think that's very sad. That area was like a little Wembley for us when we were small. I've now had the chance to play at the national stadium as a result of honing my skills in streets. I just hope that opportunity isn't going to be denied future generations by killjoys.'

Stuart Lovell – a little Wembley in Caversham Park

Lads growing up in the 1930s and 40s had little opportunity for organised football, and even footballs were hard to come by, as Norrie Hart remembers.

'My football in those days was spent with Ted Cambridge at Long Barn rec down by the Four Horseshoes off the Basingstoke Road – the Dunes we used to call them. Ted's mother saved up Oxo coupons and got a real football, a brown leather football – we'd never seen one like that to play with because Whitley kids didn't have anything.

'Ted used to go down to Long Barn rec – he lived just across the way – and with anything from eight to 25-a-side, depending on the weather, they would choose sides – Ted, because it was his ball and Eric Smith, who was later to play for Reading. That was all the football us kids had. There was no really organised football. The schools didn't have any coaches – they've probably got too many now.'

For Bill Cam and the other lads who grew up during the war years in St Andrew's Home for orphaned and homeless boys, in Wilton Road, Reading, football was their life, 'the only way

'If you didn't make the top 14 or 15 in school's football you had to spend all your time playing rounders and netball in the playground with the girls. I wasn't really old enough to know why some of the older boys got quite excited about – if you'll pardon the expression – dark blue knickers and white blouses.'

Norrie Hart

11

you could let off steam and feel free to run around'.

'We had a football and where we had been using it on the concrete it got worn out very quickly so, as the holes came, you put patches on it and in the end the ball was just patches.

'We played every Saturday and sometimes on a Sunday afternoon in the grounds on a piece of asphalt where flats have now been built. Just over the back we looked into Kensington Road recreation ground, where Huntley and Palmers played, and we used to sit on the fence watching them play. There were some nut trees nearby, and we used to eat nuts as we watched.'

It was not until Bill left the home at the end of the war that he began to play football in the streets.

'We had coats for goal-posts and plenty of arguments.'

Bill Cam

'Street football really blossomed just at the end of the war. Very few people had any footballs, and you would kick around with tennis balls or anything you could get – in fact I remember playing with a lump of coke. There weren't any organisations for playing football, and some of the parks were used for allotments so children used to play in the streets. The traffic was very sparse in those days. If you had a car you were somebody. It was mostly bicycles – but there wasn't even an abundance of those.

'What used to happen was you'd go to school and at the end of the session you would arrange to meet your mates. Then somebody else you'd know would come along and say, "Let's have a little kick around," and that's really how street football started. Other children in the road could see you playing and that would attract some more who would ask, "Can I play?" and in the end there were so many of us we had to have two teams. Invariably the one who owned the ball would be captain.

'I was living in Prince of Wales Avenue at that time but the games I remember most were in Kensington Road and Cranbury Road. You decided how long you were going to play and it was taken very seriously. Some friends would get together and pick their team and call it something – I think they went by the roads, Kensington Wanderers and Cranbury Know-alls or something – and then challenge somebody else. You had a halfway line and goals, but the kerb was as far as you could go so really you were restricted. But in those days – it was from about 1945 to 47 – it was good to be playing outside because during the war years you couldn't do that as much.

'You would have these chums who got together in a team, and there was always someone in the next street you knew with their team and it would snowball like that. After school you'd go home, get your tea and then play until it got dark. The time seemed limitless. I can't even remember turning round but I suppose we did! We wore our ordinary clothes and shoes till mothers and fathers complained. My shoes never lasted very long because I was football mad.

'We didn't get many complaints initially but it did eventually get out of hand and a few windows got broken. There was one particular lady we used to think was very nasty and she was always complaining. Unfortunately it was her window which seemed to get broken most – I don't think it was deliberate, it was just one of those things. I broke it one day. I was in the habit of kicking things along the street and I booted this stone and it hit the top of the kerb and went straight through her window. To us she was a bit of an ogre but she had good reason. We made a lot of noise shouting.

Young footballer Bill Cam (front row second from left)

'In the end, the car drivers and the cyclists got to know roughly the times when football matches were taking place and they would avoid those streets. Certainly Kensington Road and Cranbury Road were very often vacant because people knew the kids would be playing there. It was really amazing to see people park their cars at the bottom or the top of the street – they always kept away from the bit where we were playing.

'I can't remember if we limited the number of players in each side but initially we didn't. It was nothing to see a street full of kids making a lot of noise and neighbours putting their heads out and saying, "Keep away from my new door and my windows." It was good fun. Anybody could play at first, the more the merrier, but then it became more sophisticated and teams got pruned a bit.

'For me it was only a short spell of street football but when you are a kid one year playing seems a long time. Football then migrated back into the parks because by this time the allotments were gone and families could afford a ball. Eventually the same sort of thing would happen in the parks and this was what really stopped the street football.'

But football was still being played vigorously in the streets in the fifties and sixties as Roland 'Roly' Ford, now chairman of Reading Town FC, recalls.

'I was born in Whitley and went to Ashmead School. We all played football. Nowadays you don't see kids kicking about in the street but when I was about 12 I used to play for Hartland Rovers. That was just one part of Hartland Road and we used to have enough people in that little bit to get a team. They were all sorts of different ages – you could go from 10 up to 15 but you didn't care about that. You went up the road and played Foxhays Rovers, and you played Ambrook Rovers or you played Hartland United, and you would arrange it yourself. You'd

OFF SIDE

'I'll have John.'
'Right, I'll have Gavin.'
'I'll take William.'
'That leaves James and
Matthew.'
'You can have them
both.'
'No, I don't want them.
You take Matthew and
I'll have James.'
'No, you take James,
Matt can be linesman.'

And for Matthew, all of a
sudden
as expected (it's a weekly
ritual),
the sunny day with its
few comfy clouds
turns to a gaping black
pit,
and misery runs the line
with him.
        Matthew Facherty, 14

just say, "Oh! we'll see you there", and there used to be a real game.

'We would put coats down and we just played. You didn't have a referee and if the ball went out, you'd say: "It's gone out." "Nah, it ain't!" If the ball went into the goal, or what was supposed to be goal, you'd say, "No it didn't, it went over the post." It was just a game.

'Hartland Road used to be a concrete road with a tarmac beading and when it was Wimbledon, it was our tennis court. When it was football, we used to play 'kerbsy'. We'd have a tennis ball and kick it to the other side - that was our area. We played cricket as well. In those days people used to look after their properties. Even council tenants used to cut their grass and that grass was our wicket. When we wore that out, we used to move on to the next one, and the next one. We would be all over the street. You couldn't do it nowadays; Hartland Road is more like a major trunk road.'

When Roland left school he continued to play football.

'Unlike the kids now all we had was a football. We'd go down to Whitley Wood rec and we could have 15 or 16 a side. One boy would turn up and you'd say, "Kick down." The next one would turn up and you'd say, "Kick up." One lot had no shirts on and the other lot would have the shirts on – either skins or shirts. You'd start off with six-a-side but you could end up with a lot more than that. You just kept on making it longer and the pitch bigger. There never was any organised football. We were the first Sunday club in Reading, and there was no Sunday league in those days. We were called Reading Orient and if you didn't go to Ashmead School you couldn't play for us. '

For Barry Elmore, childhood football meant the Tank in Whitley Street.

'When I talk about football I immediately think back to when I was a kid. My mates and I learned our football in a place called the Tank. This was, and still is, a disused reservoir, emptied of water. It was our White Hart Lane, our Old Trafford. To play a game in the Tank meant kicking up and down slopes and hopefully ending up scoring a goal. This must have been good practice as the Tank turned out many excellent local footballers.'

Barry graduated to organised football in the shape of the Mount Pleasant Youth Club team in the Reading Nursery League.

'At the time the youth club was in Silver Street, opposite the Greyhound pub. Unfortunately for the youth of the area the Club, as we knew it, was demolished some years ago. We were the only team around with a lady as a manager. We all piled into her Austin Mayflower for away matches. Not a track suit or bench coat like managers of today, for her it was a full-length fur coat and boots. I'm sure the winters were colder then, but she was there rain or shine.'

READING SCHOOLS

by David Downs

The Reading Schools' Football Association was formed in 1894, and is one of the oldest schools' football associations in the world.

In its first season the association organised a league competition for 12 local secondary schools, and limited its activities to supervising those fixtures. A challenge cup was competed for in 1897 and, by the turn of the century, schools' football in the town was well established, with many boys playing in matches both in midweek and on Saturday mornings.

By 1904 a district representative side was fielded, and inter-league fixtures were played against Newbury, Oxford, South London, Swindon and Windsor. In the following season, Reading became a founder member of the English Schools' FA and entered the national English Schools' Shield competition.

In the first season following the Great War, Reading won the English Schools' Shield for the first and, so far, only time. In May 1920, Reading Boys defeated Grimsby Boys 1-0 in the final played at Elm Park, as a corner kick taken by Frank Eckhart (Wilson Central School) was deflected into his own net by a Grimsby defender.

Reading also reached the final in 1924, losing to North Staffs 1-0 at Stoke City's ground, the only score coming from a penalty kick just two minutes from time.

*Former schoolboy star
Frank Eckhart*

Reluctant goalkeeper

Jimmy Jones, who played in that final as goalkeeper when he was 14 years old, recalled the match vividly, although he described himself as a reluctant goalkeeper 'because I was afraid of making a mistake and letting the side down'.

In the 1923-24 season, the Coley team was a good one. In addition to Jimmy, the team also included Cherry Luckett, the captain, who, the following season, was selected to play for England Schoolboys against Wales twice and Scotland.

Coley won the Harry Childs Cup and the Rufus D Isaacs Shield, and Jones and Luckett played for Reading Boys in the English Schools Shield competition, later to be known as the Trophy.

The Schools Shield meant additional training for the lads. The Coley boys in the squad went to Palmer Park one lunchtime each week by tram, where the team managers, Jimmy Thomas and Vic Turner, put them through their paces.

The boys would take part in sprints, relay and tag races, then finish with a game while the trainers offered encouragement and advice.

Jimmy Jones also had to practise saving shots and penalties, something which was to stand him in good stead.

Then, after a quick wash and a change, it was back on the tram to Coley in time for afternoon school.

This additional training paid off, for Reading Boys progressed steadily through the early rounds of the Shield competition by defeating Bramley, Windsor, Hitchin and Tipton.

In Round Five they beat the much-fancied Bristol Boys, and were rewarded with a visit to Nottingham to watch Notts County play.

Jones was told to watch particularly the Notts County goalkeeper, Albert Iremonger, who at 6ft 5ins, was the tallest player to play professional football. He could throw the ball three-quarters of the length of the pitch.

Their win over Bristol took Reading into the quarter-final, where they beat Brighton Boys 2-0 at Elm Park after a goalless draw at Brighton, and in the semi-final they defeated Aberdare Boys 2-1, also at Elm Park, but only after a dour struggle which went into extra time.

Reading's winning goal was scored by left-winger Reg Pearce, who in later life was for over 50 years Huntley and Palmers' groundsman at their playing field in Kensington Road.

Now Reading were in the final, which in those days was decided by one game. Their opponents were North Staffs at the Stoke City ground. Reading travelled up to Stoke by train on the day before the final, but their problems began during the journey when Charlie Bidmead's thumb was trapped in a carriage door and he had to play with it in a splint.

Reading's team for the final

Reading Boys Team 1923-4 - finalists English Schools Shield. Jimmy Jones is in the middle of the centre row

was: Jones (Coley); Beale (Sutton Central); Townsend (Battle); Harding (Collier General); Withers (Redlands); Wedlock (Wilson Central); Luckett (Coley); Seward (Oxford Road); Bidmead (Sutton Central); Minter (Katesgrove); Pearce (Katesgrove).

A crowd of 21,000, almost all of them supporting the home side, saw the match at the famous Victoria Ground. Jimmy Jones recalled vividly some of the incidents that occurred during the final.

'We had a good team talk and a general gee-up from the team managers before the match. We were quite confident as we were a good team, and had an excellent team spirit. The game was very even, but then North Staffs were awarded a penalty in the first half. The first shot went over the bar, but the referee ordered it to be retaken because I had moved. This time the player shot waist-high, just to my left. I was able to grab hold of the ball and hang on.'

That save kept Reading in the game until very near the end of the match, which looked certain to go into extra time, until another misfortune befell Reading.

'It was almost time, and we were defending well, when "Chunky" Beale, our right back was considered by the referee to have handled the ball in our penalty area. "Chunky" pleaded with the referee and showed him the mark on the front of his white jersey where the ball had hit him, but the ref would have none of it, and the penalty kick was taken. This one was a real scorcher, just inside the post, and I had no chance of stopping it.'

Les Withers, who was Reading's centre-half that day, has a similar recollection of the incident.

'We were well in the game and looking forward to at least a replay until there was a heavy shower about 20 minutes from time, which made the pitch very muddy. Suddenly a high ball from one of their defenders was lofted into our penalty area, skidded as it landed, and hit "Chunky" Beale on the stomach. The referee immediately awarded a penalty, even though Beale showed him the muddy patch on his jersey. We knew the referee was wrong, and I think he may have realised it himself afterwards, because he never turned up at the dinner after the game.'

In the 1930s there was a record number of more than 40 schools entering domestic competitions, and charity matches raised considerable sums of money for the Mayor of Reading's Unemployment Fund as well as the Royal Berkshire Hospital.

17

A Junior Schools' Cup and League competition for the under-13 age group was introduced in 1935, and similar competitions for the under-11s in 1939. A London Evacuated Schools' Football Association was formed in Reading during the Second World War, and although the national Shield competition was suspended, Reading carried on with inter-school matches at all age levels.

The post-war years have seen the Reading Schools' FA experience varying fortunes, though more recent seasons have been among the most successful the Association has known.

One of the young players of recent times went on to make a name for himself in quite a different arena. Peter Glanville, a well-known local footballer who played in goal for Wokingham Town, Slough Town, Wallingford Town and Thatcham, was a teacher at Meadway School in Tilehurst, and while in charge of soccer teams there, coached a youngster named Kenneth Branagh. He recalls:

Kenneth Branagh – the play's the thing

'Ken was a very enthusiastic member of school teams at Meadway. He had a certain amount of skill, but what impressed me most was his willingness to run and chase after the ball at every opportunity. One of his best performances was as a member of the Meadway under-15 team that won the Reading Schools' five-a-side competition in 1976 by beating Bulmershe School 1-0 in the final.

'I do remember there were times when Ken could not get to practices, either because he was preparing for a school play, or rehearsing at the Progress Theatre, but you could never fault him for commitment when he was out on the field. And I can never remember him using his acting ability to try and win us a free kick or a penalty, by pretending that he had been fouled, as if he were a Macbeth or a Klinsmann.'

Kenneth continued to put acting before football and went on to become famous as a director, producer, and actor.

Famous victory

The primary schools formed their own section in 1977, with the majority of the 40 affiliated schools playing in six-a-side leagues and an 11-a-side knock-out shield competition.

The Primary Association's greatest success came in July 1983, at Wembley Stadium, when the small village school of Mortimer St Mary's, near Reading, were the winners of the ESFA/Smith six-a-side competition from an original entry of more than 6,000 schools, watched by a crowd of 46,000.

Caversham Primary School, from Reading, also achieved third place in the 1989 National Finals at Wembley.

The secondary section organises fixtures for 20 member

schools, and with this secure base, the Reading Boys team has done exceptionally well over the past 20 years in the national trophy. The quarter-finals were reached in 1975 and 1979, and in 1980 Reading were beaten finalists, losing 4-1 on aggregate to Middlesbrough Boys. In 1992 Reading were beaten semi-finalists.

The Reading Schools' Football Association currently fields representative teams at Primary (under-11), under-14 and under-15 age levels. For many years the under-15 team made an Easter tour to Malta, and the Primary team has visited Jersey for the Easter Festival of Football for the last 21 seasons.

The Reading SFA supplies many players to Berkshire County squads, at under-11, under-14, under-15 and under-18 age levels. In addition, 15 boys, winning a total of 35 caps, have represented their country in England Schoolboy International teams.

The victorious team from Mortimer St Mary's Junior School which won the ESFA/Smith six-a-side competition at Wembley on June 11, 1983. The squad was David Tuttle (captain), Donald Stanley, Justin Plank, Paul West, Darren Watson, Christopher Nixon, Graham Crichton and Daniel Cussell. David Tuttle (third from left) went on to a successful professional career and is now captain of Sheffield United.

UNIVERSITY FOOTBALL

Football enthusiasts do not, of course, leave their love of the sport behind with their schooldays. It is an interest for life which continues through college and working life. Football has always had a strong tradition at Reading University, with the students fielding several teams each Saturday, playing in a mixture of local league and national student competitions.

As University College, Reading were the winners of the Reading Town Football Challenge Cup (Wednesday Section) as long ago as 1903-04, when J F Thomas captained their team. The college repeated the feat in 1906-07, this time captained by H F Weeks.

More recently, the most notable achievement by the Reading University 1st XI was to reach the semi-final of the Universities Athletic Union Championships in 1968-69. Reading had beaten Bath, Exeter, Bristol, and the City Universities to reach the quarter-final. At that stage they defeated Manchester University 2-1 after a 3-3 draw at Reading. In the semi-final, played at Reading FC's ground, Elm Park, Reading lost 0-1 to Loughborough Colleges, a team of PE specialists who regularly made impressive progress in the FA Amateur Cup.

A CLASS OF HIS OWN
An appreciation by Bryan Horsnell

If there is one name synonymous with schools football in the Reading area it is that of David Downs

Talk to anybody in the Reading area about schools football of the past 30 years and, inevitably, the name David Downs will come up. The current Reading Primary Schools' squad is managed by David Downs and his faithful sidekick Mike Cutbush, and their names have become synonymous with schools football in the area for more than a quarter of a century.

David Downs first became involved with the Reading Boys team in 1966, when he assisted Bob Fry, a teacher at E P Collier School. At the time, David was a newly-qualified teacher at the Battle Junior School which, appropriately, was within sight and sound of his other love, Reading FC's ground at Elm Park.

After a couple of seasons with Bob Fry, he took over as team manager of the Reading Primary Schools representative side and was joined by Mike Cutbush, who now teaches at Moulsford Preparatory School.

Left to right: David Downs, Bryan Horsnell, Mike Cutbush

During the past 30 years, hundreds of boys have represented the town at under-11 level and many of those have gone on to greater things in local and professional football, even at international level. Amongst David's protegés are Steve Wicks (QPR, Chelsea and England U21), Adrian Cooper (Reading and England Boys), Neil Webb (Reading, Portsmouth, Nottingham Forest, Manchester United and England), Lawrie Sanchez (Reading, Wimbledon, Swindon, England Boys and N Ireland), Martin Allen (QPR, West Ham, Portsmouth, England

20

U21), David Tuttle (Spurs, Sheffield United, England Youth), Archie Lovell, and so the list goes on.

At the start of the 1995-96 season, David had managed the Reading Boys team in more than 980 competitive matches and by the time this book is published he will have broken the 1,000 barrier – which must be a unique achievement within the English Schools' Football Association.

In addition to being deputy head at Ranikhet Primary School and joint manager of Reading Boys, David is Secretary of Reading Primary Schools FA, a coach at Reading FC's School of Excellence, and Reading Football Club's official historian. His book, 'Biscuits and Royals, a history of Reading Football Club', is now regarded as a collectors' item.

Although he didn't achieve any great success as a player – despite the nickname 'White Pele' – David has been in love with football for as long as he can remember. He has appeared on the bench at Wembley when Mortimer St Mary's School won the ESFA Primary Schools six-a-side final, was physio to Reading Reserves on several occasions, an extra in the TV series, The Manageress, reporter and columnist to both local newspapers, and contributor to numerous club histories, Who's Whos and football yearbooks.

THE GREATEST GAME OF ALL
by Patrick Dunne

My first impression of school football was when I started school as a five-year old and I could see the juniors playing from the infant playground. It was Dominic Green who I can remember scoring a goal almost every day. I watched them dribbling and shooting, and I decided football was my game.

Because we were not allowed balls in the infant playground, I found a round stone, and started to kick it about with my friends Luke Grover and Lewis Burton. When I went into the juniors, I was a lot better and I could control the ball.

I joined in with their games, and sometimes I would get put in a team with the not-so-good players, like Daniel Atkinson and the Augustus brothers, Daniel and Richard. We were beaten almost every day; one score I can always remember was when we lost 4-25. Yes, I know we were thrashed, but I did score two of our goals, and Lewis Burton got the other two.

In my first year in the juniors, our school team won the Reading Schools Knockout Cup, beating Southcote 2-1 in the final, but I was too young to be picked for that team.

Enthusiasm for football in schools is stronger than ever, particularly when there are young players like Patrick Dunne, a 10-year-old pupil at Ranikhet Primary School, in Tilehurst

21

Patrick Dunne

When I was a Year 4 pupil, I realised that I had a good goal-keeping ability, and I played in goal a lot. I could quite easily save some of the older boys' penalty kicks, such as those taken by Christopher Allen, David and Lee Cuthbertson, Sebastian Sarmiento and Adrian Thompson. I knew how good I was; I just wished I could be a bit better out on the pitch.

When I went into Year 5, in September 1994, I knew I had a chance of being picked for the school team. In the end I made my debut against Saint Nicholas School at Newbury. We won 1-0 with Adam Osman scoring the winning goal. The pitch was astroturf, and it was like playing on ice because it was so slippery. Our next game was against Ridgeway and we won 12-0 so I didn't have much to do in goal.

I became a regular in the Ranikhet 'B' team six-a-side squad, and my best game was against English Martyrs when we won 3-1 and I saved some difficult, point-blank shots. I hate to say it but I was sick that day.

I next got selected to play in the Reading Schools Centenary Cup semi-final against St Anne's School. We won 4-1, and I was a substitute, coming on for Thomas Soares for the last five minutes. Louie Soares scored three of our goals and Luke Holloway the other one.

Now we were in the final against Long Lane School, and I was substitute again. We had drawn 2-2 with them about three months before, but this time they were too good for us, and beat us 4-1 to win the shield. Christopher Allen scored our only goal. All our 11 players, plus the two substitutes, were presented with one of the Reading Schools Centenary Medals as a souvenir for reaching the final. I was very pleased to have collected my first football medal, and all this was thanks to having watched the juniors play from the infant playground.

I think football is the greatest game of all!

Some youngsters start playing football thanks to the Cub Scouts. Many packs run a football team and, as brothers Ian and Stuart Godfrey agree, it's a great way to start playing

MY GLORIOUS SEASON
by Ian Godfrey

My introduction to the world's greatest sport came at Elm Park on March 22, 1986, when I saw the Royals beat Bury 2-0. My first chance in competitive action came when I joined the Kennet Valley Cub pack, who ran a side in the Riverside Cubs League. In that first season, 1988-89, we finished runners-up in Division 2. I had always dreamed of being a winger but found my best position was in defence.

I started out then as a left-back, and remained there in the 1989-90 season. Unfortunately fewer teams were available that

22

year as they split into two separate leagues, leaving just one division in each. This was a disappointing year as we finished seventh out of the 12 teams. We did reach the semi-finals of the six-a-side competition though. Sixteen sides started but it was while in the last four that we became victims of the dreaded penalty shoot-outs and bowed out 4-3. However this was the first time I had captained a team and it gave me a lot more confidence in myself going into my final season.

1990-91 – our dream season. Training was never a very big part of Cubs' football and we had just two sessions before the kick-off of our assault on the league title. Our first match was away though, against one of the top teams, Sulhampstead and Ufton Nervet. Without our main striker we struggled to a 2-2 draw on a bumpy surface. But after that we never looked back, winning every game by margins of anything from 4-1 in the last league game of the season to 26-0!

However Sulhampstead did not lose either and so the league was shared, despite our vastly superior goal difference. And a week later we were going for the 'double'. It was the cup final against 79th Chippewa. I was fortunate enough to be captain, and we turned on the style, fighting back from 1-0 down early on to lead 2-1 at the break and eventually win 4-1. I even managed to score our second, coming from left-back to chip in the goal which turned the tide in our favour.

But that was not quite the end of my most glorious season. Four days later, whilst playing for Kennet Valley School, we fought back from 2-0 down at half-time against Francis Bailey to win the Bill McIlvride cup 3-2. We even missed a penalty at 2-1! Unfortunately this was my last year for both the Cubs and the school, but what a way to finish!

BEATING TORNADO
by Stuart Godfrey

My first game in Cubs' foothball was at Burghfield against 63rd Tornado. We won 3-0. This first season we did very well as we lost only two matches and our cup run was fantastic. We got to the semi-final where we beat 79th Chippewa 3-2 and so went into the final to play 63rd Tornado. We won 4-0 thanks mainly to a hat-trick from David Bramley. It poured with rain the whole time but I enjoyed my first cup final on May 9 1992.

The following season we stopped playing at Burghfield and switched to Kennet Valley School. I moved from right back to central defence. As a result of the age restrictions we lost about seven players. In the first game of the new season we had to play 79th Chippewa at their ground, Victoria rec in Tilehurst. Unfortunately we lost 6-4 but it was a wonderful game. In our first home game of the 1992-93 campaign Damien Pridham scored both goals as we defeated 63rd Tornado 2-1.

The following week we travelled to Sulhampstead. In the middle of the match two horses wandered on to the pitch! Some strange things happen from time to time. Another example is my first goal. It was whilst playing 79th Commanche that our attack broke down and the cleared ball fell to me on the half-way line. I ran forward a few yards and then struck it hard along the ground. None of the opposition could get to it and it somehow squeezed through the crowded penalty area. The goalkeeper was over the other side and could not prevent a stunning goal! We ended up finishing seventh that year with our new striker Daniel Parfitt scoring 20 goals in the process.

The following season, my last, I formed a centre back partnership with Matthew Knight under the command of our joint managers, John Godfrey and Mike Parfitt. We were also presented with a new kit courtesy of Thames Valley Engraving and Steve Green Design.

We finished fifth in the league behind the winners, 79th Chippewa. We had a good cup run though, beating 63rd Tornado 2-0 to reach the semi-finals but losing 2-1 to 80th Reading. However I was in the Kennet Valley school team which won the Bill McIlvride cup, beating Francis Bailey 1-0.

Cubs' football is a great way to start playing.

A GOAL TO REMEMBER
by Daniel Bamford

Even the more unorthodox goals can provide moments of glory according to Daniel Bamford of Class 6L, at Westwood Farm County Junior School

It was a Saturday at Denefield School and the pitch was wet. The match was against Loddon Valley Rangers and I was playing for Westwood Wanderers. I was playing right back and in the first five minutes they had all the possession. About a minute later they scored. It was 2-0 at half time.

In the second half they scored straight after kick-off. They scored again about five minutes later. After our kick-off Antony O'Connor got kicked in the knee so lots of men came on the pitch arguing over whether the culprit should be sent off. I didn't know what was going on so I sat down.

After about five minutes of arguing, the game was back on. Ten minutes later they came on the attack, I stuck my leg out and scored an own goal. Then the whistle blew.

Everyone said it was a good goal. Well, it was.

2 Mud, Sweat and Beer

The grassroots of local football

by Duncan Mitchell

At first glance, Reading might not be considered as a major centre of footballing excellence. For a town of its size it has a record of under-achievement at professional level and, certainly in recent years, has failed to produce a team that could be thought of as a major force in the non-league/semi-professional ranks. But if you dig a little deeper, great names of former years are revealed, along with recollections of huge crowds and unbeatable teams until it appears that the town has overflowed with talent and top level competition. Facts, though, speak for themselves, and the fact is that Reading has always been a football crazy town.

Praise must go to the men and women of the town who ensure that competition exists within the area. Without their dedication the century of local football which provides the memories and stories that follow would never have been possible. People such as Ray Stroomer, Cyril Towner, Norrie Hart, Ted Cambridge, John Waters, to name but a few, have all committed their time to ensuring young lads throughout the area have been able to enjoy the 'beautiful game'. There have been many equally dedicated people before them and we can only hope there will be many more to follow.

The shape of local football changes at an alarming rate with teams folding, forming and reforming each new season. As a result, tracing the history of many clubs becomes an almost impossible task and to add to the confusion teams have begun to use sponsors' names as their own club name. On top of this there are regular ground changes, colour changes and the introduction in recent years of Sunday sides bearing the same names as their Saturday counterparts but registering as entirely different clubs.

Competitive football has been played in Reading since 1891 with the formation of the Reading Temperance League, which in later years was to become the Reading and District League.

Starting with just a single division, the founder members competed for a solid silver trophy, donated by a Mr Fidler, a representative of the local corn and seed merchants. The very first winners, in the 1891-92 season, were Castle Institute. Their

'About the same number of people play in Saturday and Sunday football as watch the Royals. We have 5,500 registered footballers for Sunday mornings; the Saturday competition has got about 3,000.'
                                    Norrie Hart

'We didn't have the television, we didn't have the nightclubs, so local football had so much support. Everybody knew everybody else and it was absolutely wonderful. We used to finish playing football on a Saturday teatime and I used to count the hours to next Saturday.'
                                    Jack Jarvis

25

1898-99 saw the first win by one of Reading's most famous clubs, Huntley and Palmers

initial success was short lived and for the following three seasons Redlands became the champions. Abbey won the title in 1895-96 before Old Kendricks began a brief domination with two successive title wins. The 1898-99 season saw the emergence of one of Reading's most famous clubs. Huntley and Palmers, then still known as Reading Biscuit Factory, won the first of their many honours that season, in what was their very first year of competitive football.

The club soon became the envy of sides from across the area and was able to run not only a first XI but also a reserve team, an 'A' team and a minor side. The team originally played on a pitch at Kings Meadow, close to the site of the Nurdin and Peacock building, before moving to the Kensington Road pitch, widely regarded as the best in Reading.

By the 1950s Huntley and Palmers had become a major force in amateur football, the like of which the town has not seen since. They had progressed to the Spartan League, one of the top amateur leagues of the day, where they competed with the likes of Marlow, Wycombe Wanderers, Hounslow and Harrow. Sadly, Huntley and Palmers did not continue as successfully as these clubs, most of which are still playing in the upper echelons of semi-professional football.

By the 1970s Huntley and Palmers were back in the Reading and District League. Unable to support the same number of teams as before because of the reduction in the size of the workforce, the club began to field players who had little or no connection with the factory and the company withdrew financial support from the football club.

By the 1980s the team's decline from the heady days of the 1950s culminated in its closure. There followed rumours that West Reading, by then the top side in Reading, were to take over at Kensington Road. The intention was for them to have their own ground which would enable them to progress, like Huntley and Palmers before them, to a higher grade of football. Plans were thwarted though when the stand at the side of the ground and the clubhouse were burned down.

From its heyday in the 1950s, the Huntley and Palmers team declined until it was forced to close in the 1980s due to lack of financial support

THE TEMPERANCE LEAGUE

With the interest generated by the newly-formed Temperance League, several new clubs were formed and as a result more competitions were introduced. The Tilehurst Charity Cup was first contested in 1896 and a second knockout competition, the Reading Challenge Cup, started the following year. In addition a Wednesday League had been formed. This was mainly made up of works teams whose employees enjoyed ·half-day closing on Wednesdays but were unable to play in the Saturday League. The Wednesday League table in January of 1898 looked like this:

The Temperance League sparked a new interest in local football

	Pld	W	L	D	F	A	Pts
1 Swifts	8	8	0	0	32	4	16
2 YMCA	10	5	4	1	30	24	11
3 Post Office	6	5	1	0	19	7	10
4 Newbury Wednesday	6	2	3	1	24	16	5
5 Acadians	6	1	5	0	8	14	2
6 Manchester House	4	0	3	1	4	18	1
7 Avondale	6	0	5	1	3	37	1

Not only do the team names of this era appear unfamiliar but so does the style of match reporting. Here is a piece taken from the Berkshire Chronicle of January 1898 involving a match between Defiance and Emmer Green:

This game was played on the Defiance ground on Saturday and a good game was witnessed.. Defiance led at half time by one to nil, Murray obtaining the point; but on the restart Perrin equalised.. Play became of an exciting character, and again Defiance obtained the lead, through Stanley. Emmer Green now played up strongly, and scoring by C and J Perrin were victorious by three goals to two.

By 1905 a second division had been added to the Temperance League and some new names had come to the fore. The town's top sides at the turn of the century were Grovelands, Central, Caversham Rovers and Wokingham Athletic.

In 1910 a couple of the local clubs found themselves in finan-cial difficulty. It wasn't just the smaller clubs that were floun-dering; Reading FC themselves were almost closed down that year, just 39 years after their formation. Faced with relegation to the second division of the Southern League, the club held an important meeting of shareholders to decide whether to con-tinue. The club were not keen to compete in Division Two but if fewer than 10 teams started the following season in Division One, Reading could obtain re-election. However, if they were to continue, financial support was urgently required. Eventually they decided to continue and a fundraising scheme was introduced with money received from the Boy Scouts' col-lection, a rummage sale, and an organ recital as well as dona-tions from other clubs including Fulham, West Ham, Swindon, and ironically, given their own current plight, Newbury.

At the turn of the century, Reading's top clubs included Caversham Rovers and Wokingham Athletic

Reading weren't alone in their troubles. In the same week Grovelands were forced to play their last home game on a pitch that the council had earmarked for use as allotments.

In the 1920s the popularity of football in the town had increased dramatically. Two more divisions were added to the Temperance League and in 1922 a second league, the Reading and District Institute League, was formed. The first meeting was held on July 17 1922. The 20 clubs who expressed an interest in joining were divided into two divisions. The teams that made up the A Section were Beech Hill, Whitley Hall, Redlands, Castle Street, Grovelands, Burghfield Reserves, ReRaOC, Grazeley, Reading Insurance, and St Paul's. The B Section teams were Mapledurham, Caversham Albions, Caversham Old Boys, Old Wilsonians, Shinfield Reserves, West Reading, Elm Park Hall, Holy Trinity, Seven Bridges, St George's.

A month later an application from Sindlesham was accepted and they also competed in the League's inaugural season. Several of these clubs already had sides playing in the older Temperance League and began to run reserve sides which they entered into the Institute League. Until 1989 when the two leagues joined, there was a widely held view that the Temperance league (Reading and District) was the stronger of the two. There are however, plenty of people who reject this claim and are quick to point out that the Institute League regularly beat the Reading and District League at representative level.

*A regular member of the
Old Wilsonians side at
the time was Arthur
Negus, famous in later
life as an antiques expert
on the BBC Television's
Going for A Song*

JOHN WATERS AND THE INSTITUTE LEAGUE

One of the people responsible for the administration of the Institute League is John 'Bunny' Waters, who, along with Bert Newman, transformed the league from the second class status with which it had been branded. In 1963 the name was changed to the Reading Combination League. A league cup competition was introduced as well as an All Champions Cup, for which the winners of the respective divisions would compete against each other for the overall Combination title. An annual six-a-side competition was also introduced, one of the few that existed at the time, and took place on Courage's sports ground, off Berkeley Avenue.

Bert was also the man behind the Allied Counties competition, a tournament that brought together league representative teams from Wycombe, Swindon, Middlesex, North Berks, East Berks, Hampshire, Andover and Basingstoke leagues in addition to the two Reading leagues. The Combination league lifted the trophy for two successive years right at the beginning of the 1970s, beating the Reading and District team by four goals to one in one of the finals, which was played at Elm Park. As well as their two victories the Combination side shared one title and were runners-up once to the Wycombe League before the competition ceased.

John Waters is one of the often underrated people who ensure that the opportunity exists for the town's young men to play football. He has been involved with the Combination league, often to the detriment of his family life, since 1963. He began his playing days with his works team, Rightform, in the Institute Leauge. He then joined Earley United Minors in the late 1930s and was a member of the victorious side of 1939-1940 which won the Berks and Bucks Minor Cup, beating Wolverton BR 3-2.

Earley missed out on a remarkable treble that year. They were pipped for the Reading Minor league title by Battle Athletic, and were also narrowly defeated in the Reading Minor Cup Final by Huntley and Palmers.

At the start of the war John played briefly for Reading's reserve team and upon return from the services joined East Reading Adult School FC (ERAS). (ERAS themselves had enjoyed a fruitful period during the 1930s with Berks and Bucks Junior Cup wins in 1930-1931 and 1934-35.) Although not actually a former prisoner of war himself, John then played briefly with an outfit called Ex-POWs which effectively was an ex-servicemen's team. In 1957 he began refereeing and officiated in many local cup finals at Elm Park before graduating to the Isthmian and Spartan leagues. John was 30 years old when he began refereeing and by the time he had worked his way to Isthmian standard was considered too old for further promotion to the Football League itself, a ruling that still rankles with him.

After many years of service to the Combination League, John finally stood down from office with the coming together of the two Reading leagues in 1989. However, he was the man behind the creation of the Reading Indoor league, a five-a-side tournament which he formed back in 1968 along with Ray Stroomer and Len Forbes, with the help of the Mormon church in the Meadway at Tilehurst.

The clubs that formed the first indoor league were:-Redlands, Redfield, Evening Post, Cotswold, Maiden Erleigh,

John Waters was 30 years old when he began refereeing and by the time he had worked his way to Isthmian standard was considered too old for further promotion to the Football League itself, a ruling that still rankles with him

Mormon Church, Henley YMCA, SEB, Clifton Athletic and Earley Rovers. Of these, SEB are the only side still involved in the evening competition. In the 27 years of its being, John has missed just three nights. The tournament is still going strong with 19 teams participating in last season's competition.

Back in the Temperance league of the 1920s Redlands and British Workman Institute (BWI) had emerged as the two dominant forces. It was decided that a premier section to the league should be formed in time for the beginning of the 1923-24 season. This élite section was to consist of a minimum of ten clubs. It was also proposed that the league name should be changed from Temperance to the Reading and District. It was anticipated that the following clubs would join the premier section: Cowley (Oxford), Newbury Town, Abingdon Town, Redlands, BWI, Maidenhead Reserves, Abingdon Pavlova, Reading Biscuit Factory, Thatcham, Henley Town, Stokenchurch and Reading Comrades.

Reading football in the 1920s was dominated by Redlands and BWI, two of the teams who joined the newly-created premier section of the Temperance League

By 1935 the balance of power had once again shifted. Since the formation of the competition no one team seemed able to dominate for any great length of time. In the early part of the decade ERAS just about held the lead over local rivals East Reading. The two of them were leading a very competitive division that by today's standards reads like some kind of Berks and Oxon 'Superleague'. It included Thatcham, Abingdon Town, Newbury Town, Wallingford, and Morris Motors (Oxford), all of whom later became Hellenic league clubs, as well as Caversham Athletic, Wargrave, Sonning and Reading Biscuit Factory.

Division Two also contained some illustrious names including Didcot Town, Wokingham, Simonds Athletic and Binfield along with some less familiar sides that have since disappeared; Old Wilsonians, Theale Comrades, Berkshire Nomads and Calcot Park.

The top Institute teams of the time included Kidmore End, St George's and Caversham Institute in Division One, with Shinfield, Thorneycrofts and Reading Central leading the way in the second division.

THE WEDNESDAY LEAGUE

The Wednesday league had by this time gained a reputation as being of an exceptionally high standard. Very few of its founder members were still competing and teams from further afield were now taking part. Enough teams had become affiliated to support a second division.

The final league tables for the 1934-35 season looked like this:

	Pld	W	L	D	F	A	Pts
1 Matthews	22	19	1	2	102	18	40
2 Tramways	22	14	3	5	63	40	33
3 Imperial	22	13	3	6	69	51	32
4 Tilehurst Wednesday	22	12	5	5	68	35	29
5 Wallingford Wednesday	22	10	9	3	52	57	23
6 RCS	22	9	9	4	40	59	22
7 Newbury Wednesday	22	8	10	4	52	46	20
8 St Bartholomews	22	7	9	6	47	54	20
9 Didcot Wednesday	22	8	11	3	56	69	19
10 Newsagents	22	6	13	3	50	63	15
11 GPO	22	4	17	1	42	73	9
12 Wokingham Wednesday	22	0	20	2	18	103	2

The Division Two results were: St Mark's 32 points from 18 matches, Twyford and Ruscombe 24, Bee's Sports 23, GWR 20, Frost's Butchers 19, Crowthorne Wednesday 15, Wednesday Athletic 15, Sandhurst Wednesday 15, Emerson and Channin 9, Bracknell Wednesday 4.

BATTLE ATHLETIC

It was during this period that the much-celebrated Battle Athletic were formed by 'Pop' Parsons and Charlie Kearse. Danny Webb, a former Battle player, recalls:

'Pop Parsons kept a shop in Cranbury Road, a little general shop, a sweet shop. What really started it off was that all the boys used to congregate outside this shop, kicking the ball about on the path, up the alleyway, and they decided to form a football team. Charlie Kearse had all the know-how, and he had a lot of connections, and so we went in the old minor league.'

In 1932 Battle Athletic was born. The club began by playing in friendly matches but within three years they had entered the Reading Minor League. They finished third in their first season and reached the semi-final stages of the Minor Cup.

Three well-known local personalities, Fred May, Maurice Love and Lionel Gibbs lent their support and the following season saw the club begin their relentless pursuit of local honours. They not only won the Minor league, dropping just one point all season at the hands of Huntley and Palmers Minors, but also secured the Reading Minor and Berks and Bucks Minor Cups, coming from behind to win in both finals, and becoming the first minor team to win the treble.

Many of Battle's players during these formative years had

Pop Parsons who died in 1972

graduated from the Battle School XI, who themselves had won the Reading Schools Shield for three consecutive years prior to Athletic's emergence. The following season another new XI retained the Minor league and also reached the Berks and Bucks final again, this time though, going down 3-1 to Wolverton. They had become known as 'the wonder team of Junior Football' and were invited to play in exhibition matches overseas. It is hard to believe that a Reading side from Prospect Park could become known throughout Europe, but this was an indication of just how strong football in the Reading area had become.

In 1937 Battle formed a Youth side that also enjoyed immediate success by winning the Youth Cup and finishing as runners-up in their league. In 1939 Huntley and Palmers crushed Battle 5-1 to send them to their first league defeat in three years.

Battle's original pitch was on the south side of Prospect Park in front of the Mansion House. From here it moved to the Bowling Green pitch, to the west of the park, which in later years was used by another of Reading's revered clubs, West Reading. From here Battle secured the use of the Palmer Park track ground (now the Stadium), which they shared with ERAS.

Battle continued to play throughout the war years as their players were too young to be called up for military service. Training took place at Elm Park and with many of Reading's players away at war some of the Battle players got the opportunity to play for the Royals' reserve or 'A' teams. Battle's ties with Elm Park grew over the years and by 1950 Mr E Carter, then chairman of Reading, became president of Battle and the club officially became the nursery club to Reading FC.

The war years gave unexpected opportunities to the young footballers of the town

A number of Battle players eventually became regulars at Elm Park such as Vic Niblett, Les Andrews, Arthur Summerfield, Eric Smith and Sylvan Anderton. Those who didn't progress to Reading's books remained loyal to Battle for many years. Jim Hughes, Laurie Crawshaw, Syd Keatley, Bill Hughes, Eddie Lawrence, Len Abery, Fred Randall, Alan Hedgington, Ron Barrett and Danny Webb were all members of the great side of 1936, while other longtime players included Johnny Leach, Fred Rolfe, Bobby Maybanks and Ken Cope.

After the war Battle Athletic became a senior side and won the Reading and District League's Premier Division twice and also the Reading Senior Cup. Some of their players were selected for Berks and Bucks teams.

Dennis 'Danny' Webb played for over 20 years and set goalscoring records by the dozen including 10 strikes in a 22-0 drubbing of Waltham St Lawrence. On returning from the war, Danny began playing for the Borough Police in the Wednesday league. By now this contained both works teams and service teams from the area, including REME Aborfield, RAF Bracknell, RAF Shinfield, RAF Danesfield, Royal Berkshire Regiment, Crowthorne Fire Service and Borough's arch rivals County Police.

The Police teams enjoyed some glorious years in the Wednesday League, with the Borough side winning just about everything in sight in the late 40s and early 50s before County Police began to challenge for supremacy. The County Police side became very strong and were one of the better sides in the Police inter-counties matches. The fact that the Borough Police and teams like Tilehurst Wednesday and Shop Assistants remained competitive while many of the county constabularies failed, shows the strength of competition in local soccer.

A great interest in the Wednesday league developed in the 1950s and many of the townspeople would spend their free Wednesday afternoons watching one of the big matches of the week. It was not unusual for two or three hundred to turn up at Tilehurst Wednesday and there were often double that at Palmer Park, where Co-op played

READING AND DISTRICT LEAGUE

By the start of the 1953-54 season there was great concern that the Reading and District league had been significantly weakened by the defection of many clubs to the newly-formed Hellenic League. The clubs that were wealthy enough to have their own grounds had begun to object to playing on park pitches and claimed that the poor quality pitches often led to their downfall. They were also ambitious enough to want to progress to a league that took in the top sides from Wiltshire and Buckinghamshire as well as from Berkshire and Oxfordshire The clubs that left were Wallingford, Thatcham, Henley Town, Morris Motors and Didcot Town.

For a few seasons the honours in Reading were spread between Tilehurst (one of Reading's oldest clubs, formed in 1896), Woodley and Elgar Rovers. Any fears that the standard of football had slipped since the formation of the Hellenic league stopped when West Reading emerged as a regular entrant in the League's honours list. Having won the Reading and District Premier division in 1955-56 as West Reading Athletic they began a remorseless pursuit of silverware that saw them land the premier division again in 1961-62. They went on to win a further seven times out of the following ten seasons. On top of this impressive list they also won the Berks and Bucks Intermediate Cup.

OLD ADVERSARIES

It is a widely accepted fact that the golden age of football existed from the 1950s to the mid-1970s. This was certainly the case for Reading.

Two sides were particularly prominent from 1959 to 1973 - West Reading and Rabson Rovers. Their rivalry had no historical or territorial origins. The teams' competitiveness grew from both clubs' superb playing records and the fact that for those 14 years there was rarely another team vying for honours with them. Only one team could become 'top dogs' of Reading and it was left to these two to battle it out. Very few players from the west of the town ever ventured south for their football, with the notable exception of Dave Chard and the Bampton twins, Terry and Tony. Despite being Whitley boys and supporters of Rabsons as young lads, the Bamptons played for West Reading in their heyday. Terry Bampton recalls the reason for their choice:

'We didn't know West Reading, we didn't know who they were, and we didn't know how good they were. All we knew was that they wore nice yellow shirts and they played in the same league. It sounds corny but it's true. It was just then that the side was beginning to take off and people used to say to me, "You're a medal hunter, that's all you are", and I said, "Well, I've only ever played for one team." I'd never played for anybody else, so I played 14 years for West Reading.'

Players and spectators alike can vividly remember huge crowds on the touchline of the bowling green pitch on Prospect Park, West's home pitch, while thousands of people used to pour on to Rabson rec for the return fixtures. Peter Bartlett, a former West Reading player, recalls:

A contemporary Areff cartoon of West Reading showing the team line-up

'In that period, the rivalry between West and Rabsons did grip the town, so much so that when we were playing Rabsons at Prospect Park once, Reading FC advertised that they would give the scores from that-

Jackie Dave Tony Dave Ray Terry Pete Tony Dave Mick Gordon
JARVIS BURBEDGE LAWRENCE BUNCH BALL BAMPTON BARTLETT BAMPTON CHARD WELLS SMITH

match every 20 minutes so it wouldn't affect their gates.'

West Reading were the elder of the two sides and had been involved in competitive football for some 20 years before Rabson's foundation in 1942. West Reading, like Battle Athletic before them, was mainly made up of local lads who were raised from three or four streets just off the Oxford Road. Despite the advances of many senior clubs in the area, these lads remained loyal to their club and saw them become a major force of local football throughout the Berks and Bucks region.

In the mid-60s and early 70s they conquered all who stood before them. Tilehurst, Woodley and Reading Exiles all boasted talented sides around this time, but it was only Rabsons that truly competed with the might of West Reading. They won the first of their five Berks and Bucks Intermediate Cups in 1964-65, by which time Rabsons had already triumphed twice (1959-60 and 1963-64), but were prevented from a monopoly of the competition by the ruling that winners of the Intermediate Cup faced automatic entry to the Senior Cup the following season and were precluded from entering the Intermediate Competition.

Consequently Wests were never able to defend their title but performed beyond all expectation whenever they were pitched into the Senior Cup. No side has enjoyed the same amount of success when making the transition from Intermediate to Senior competition and many well-established senior teams had their reputations dealt a severe blow at the hands of West Reading. Having defeated teams of the calibre of Thatcham, Wallingford Town, Beaconsfield and Aylesbury, Wests would return to the Intermediate Cup every other year and walk away with it as a matter of course.

'There was such rivalry! Years later, when I was playing with the kids, if there were coloured counters, I would always choose yellow - I wouldn't have red because that was Rabsons colours.'
Peter Bartlett

The Rabson Rovers line-up depicted by Areff

— RABSON ROVERS —

Les   Alan   Gordon   Jeff   Micky   Andy   Lal   Len   Peter   Phil   Spike
WEST BUTCHER WILKINSON ROOTHAM CLIFFORD ALLEYNE DURDEN HICKS LORD FARMER GARDNER

35

*'The swinging sixties
were fine because the
lads used to spend all
evening talking about
football and the wives
and the girls used to be
going mad.'*

Jack Jarvis

The Rabson Rovers honours list makes enviable reading. Along with the Berks and Bucks wins in 1959-60 and 1963-64 Rabsons also captured the Reading and District Premier League Championship in 1964-65, 1967-68 and 1978-79, by which time they had won their third Intermediate Cup. This was backed up with Reading Senior Cups in 1963-64 and 1964-65. Despite all this success Rabsons remained, in the words of Dave Jeanes, a former Rovers goalkeeper, 'always the brides-maid, never the bride'.

The players of the two sides became local celebrities and were recognised throughout the town in a way that is now reserved only for the full-time professionals at Reading. Bill Maule, Dave Burbedge, Dave Chard, Pete Bartlett, Jack Jarvis, Micky Wells at West Reading and Jack Ingram, Barry Humphries, Lal Durden, Ray 'Sam' Maynard at Rabsons, are all to this day well remembered by fooball-loving people around the town.

Dave Chard is recalled with particular fondness, especially for his captaincy skills. Jack Jarvis, a fellow team member, is one of his many admirers:

'Dave Chard was captain of the football club. Even today everybody talks about him as the finest captain you will ever see. He never ever criticised a player, he just gave everybody encouragement. He was a fantastic captain.

Jack remembers one particular event that demonstrates Dave Chard's legendary loyalty to his team.

'We were playing Rabsons and Dave got a real nasty smack on the leg. We could not get Dave off, so we strapped him up. This was in the first half. He could hardly walk but he played for the whole of the ninety minutes. They took him to hospital after the game, and he had a broken leg. That's David , say no more.'

By the mid-60s competition had grown so great that in one campaign the two sides met in the penultimate game of the

*Crowds were packed four deep
when West Reading played
Rabsons in the 60s*

season with Rabsons just one point clear from Wests at the top of the table. An enormous crowd of 2,500 people streamed on to Rabsons rec and were four deep in places around the edge of the pitch. They watched West Reading snatch an 88th minute winner from Dave Burbedge to win the game 2-1. The following week they won the title. Tony Bampton recalls:

A Dave Burbedge goal captured by Areff

'That was the game we all remember more than any, not only because we won, but because it was just such a fantastic evening. I would say most of us, certainly Dave Burbedge and one or two others, were sick in the dressing room, sick at work, we were very, very nervous. It was a good game. It's easy saying it when you've won, but it really was a good game.'

In the 1967-68 season the two clubs tied for the Reading and District Premier League and met in a play-off at Elm Park in May 1968. This time Rabsons won the game. More people watched this game than watched Reading's last home game of the season the following weekend!

The stars of those games can remember many meetings between the two clubs and every time they came up against each other, hundreds, if not thousands would be in attendance. They can recall occasions when the ball would go out for a throw-in. Because the spectators were not willing to lose the vantage point they had gained for themselves, none of them were willing to fetch the ball. The players had to fight their way through the crowds, and return not knowing exactly where the throw-in should be taken from. The crowds were so thick, they would end up taking the throw-in at a point in the crowd which was easiest to break through.

The players of that golden era all agree that football in the area has declined ever since the two sides began to age and the younger players were unable to carry on with the good work. Some even say that local football died in 1968, on the night of the Elm Park play-off – the standard by then was so good and the excitement so intense that the only way from there was down. The decline has continued, although West Reading continue to play in the Premier Division, but Rabson Rovers have sadly slipped down to Division One (Kennet), which is, in effect, the third division of the Saturday league.

SUNDAY LEAGUE

During the West Reading/Rabsons period of glory a major development in the local soccer scene was taking place.

Reading Sunday League begun in 1964 - the first winners were the Royal Berkshire Regiment

Although competitive football had been played in the town as long ago as 1891, a Sunday League was not formed until 1964. There was, though, a Sunday knockout competition in existence before this date while Reading Wanderers and Reading Orient had been playing in the already well established Maidenhead Sunday League. However, Reading Orient did not join the Sunday League in Reading when it was first formed. Its founder members were: Royal Berks TA, Reading Transport, Ampex, Clifton Athletic, Balmore Sports, Gowrings, Ayres, Joynes, Mapledurham United, Unicorn, Reading Thistle, Reading Garage, St Michael's, and the previous season's Sunday Cup winners, Slumberland.

Royal Berks were everyone's favourites to win the title. They had in previous years played invitation matches against other service sides in Germany and had won various tournaments throughout the UK. Their captain was the highly-regarded Brian Gutteridge, a regular in Newbury's first team. The first round of matches got under way on September 6, 1964, and Ayres were first to top the table following a 7-1 demolition of Transport.

The following season the size of the Sunday League increased when, amongst others, Torpedo and Theale, Reading's most successful Sunday club, joined ranks. Theale's Saturday side was as old as any in Reading having been formed in 1884. Success for the club has been sporadic on Saturdays although they have won honours in both the Reading and District and Institute Leagues. In the early 1960s they had a particularly good team and fielded well-known local players Keith Eatwell and Tony Caswell, both of whom went on to have trials with numerous professional clubs. Dover Athletic snapped up Keith and even paid for him to travel down to Kent each week to play.

Theale's Sunday side, though, have been an almost permanent fixture near the top of the Senior division. Without doubt their greatest honour and the most prestigious trophy ever to be won by a Reading team came when they clinched the FA Sunday Cup, the only national Sunday competition, at Elm Park in May 1992. In recent seasons Reading's representatives in the FA Sunday Cup have included Theale, Reading Borough, who reached the semi-finals in 1993, Courage, Caversham Park and Thorn Walk Tavern.

Merging of the leagues

Coming right up to date, the merger of the Combination and

Reading and District leagues saw the coming together of 165 years of Saturday football. In recognition of this event a match took place between representatives of the two leagues at Palmer Park Stadium on August 28, 1989. Royal Mail were the representatives of the Reading and District league while Cookham Dean played under the Combination flag as one of the league's most successful sides over the preceding years.

THAMES VALLEY CHURCHES LEAGUE

There is only one football league where players are marked for fair play, where blasphemy is a sending-off offence and 50 per cent of the team has to be churchgoers – the Church League. There are leagues all over the country and the local one, Thames Valley Churches Football League, which consists of 12 teams, covers the greater Reading area, spreading as far as West London. An ecumenical league with teams from Anglican, Baptist and Free churches, it has been going for more than 10 years. Teams play on Saturday mornings – no Sunday matches for them.

In the Church League the football managers, captains and 50 per cent of each squad have to be churchgoers

There is no denying that the football league is an evangelical ploy to attract more people into the church but it is also a way of giving churchgoers who enjoy their football a chance to play the game with the right Christian spirit.

Andy Brown, manager of the Greyfriars team, who has been involved in the league for five years as player and referee, says, 'It is an opportunity to play football in an environment that's a bit friendlier than in normal leagues. People do enjoy this friendliness and the better behaviour of these games.'

To deflect criticism that people might come along only for the football and forget the church, the league rules say that the manager, captain and 50 per cent of the squad have to be church members.

'They aren't vetted strictly because we go on trust,' said Andy. 'We don't ask for written proof from a minister; we rely on the discretion of the individual churches.'

The league is not affiliated to the FA either locally or nationally because there are slightly different rules; the 50 per cent requirement, minor rules on substitution, and the attitude towards blasphemy. 'Anyone in any league who uses the f-word should get a booking, but a player in our league who takes the name of the Lord in vain – God or Christ – is much-more likely to get a booking or even be sent off than in a normal game. It's the churches' responsibilty to warn their players about the blasphemy rule and those who object don't play.'

There is also a fair play league to encourage teams to play in the right spirit. At each game the referee marks the team out of 10 on their sportsmanship and behaviour and phones in this mark with the results each week. The team with the highest score at the end of the season wins a shield; teams which regularly score below six have to answer a few searching questions. Potentially they could be thrown out of the league though it hasn't happened yet.

There is a wide range of abilities in each team. 'You get people who have played at quite a decent level, and people who can just about stand on one leg – like me,' said Andy. 'There are no particularly good teams.

'We want to be unlike other leagues, with a good attitude on the pitch. It's an extension of Christianity, we want to be different from the world around.'

Some teams in the Church League have decided to take their chances in the outside world. One of the Thames Valley teams, Wycliffe, opted out three years ago and joined the Reading League. While maintaining their standards of behaviour and their 50 per cent churchgoers squad, they have still managed to climb from the fourth to third dvision.

And has football attracted many players from the pitch to the pew? 'I have heard of people who have been drawn into the church because of their involvement in the Church League,' said Andy.

"Do all to the glory of God"

3 Around the Clubs

Notable local sides

by Duncan Mitchell

There are almost 200 clubs competing in either the Reading Saturday or Sunday League, many of which run two or even three teams. Some clubs disband, then return under a different name in a different division, but there are several noteworthy clubs in existence which have been running for many years.

THAMES VALE FC

This club was formed in 1938 by a group of friends from the Norcot Estate who used to kick a ball around on a piece of land by the river, at the bottom of Scours Lane. The three founder members were Bill Rogers, Ron North, and Percy Ford. Their first game was at Frilsham, where they won a friendly match against the village side by 10 goals to four.

Vale entered the Reading and District League in 1946, winning their first game 7-1 against St Bart's with Frank George scoring the club's first league goal.

Fred Millard joined the club in 1947 and helped to run the reserve team which entered the Institute League in the 1947-48 season. Fred has remained with the club ever since and has spent many years as vice president. He went on to run the line for the first XI and continued until he was 64. Fred and his wife Betty are still watching Vale play and whatever the weather can be seen on the touchline of pitch number two on Prospect Park. Since they first became involved, Fred and Betty have missed no more than a dozen first team games.

The club began its most fruitful spell in the early 60s and won the Berks and Bucks Junior Cup in 1973-74, to date the club's greatest honour. During their glory years the team was run by Ken Jones and included fine players like Don Leeke, Pete Beere, Ray Newport and Den Bull as well as Roy Barrington and Jim White, who still share the club goalscoring record of 62 goals in a season.

The club remains very much a family affair. Not only are Fred and Betty Millard still heavily involved, but their daughter, the current club secretary, is married to former player and current chairman Ray Crawshaw. Nephew Andy North played for many years and their grandson Ian is the current team manager.

Betty Millard, Ron North's sister, can remember watching many of Vale's early matches. She recalls one match away to St Benedict's, the borstal, where the inmates were more interested in ogling Betty and her friend than they were in watching the match. Mrs Millard might well regret ever having been persuaded to attend the game - she's been washing Vale's kit ever since!

Peter Beere by Areff

41

SEB (READING) FC

Founded in 1954 by a group of football enthusiasts from the SEB offices in Market Place, the club began in Division Four of the Institute League and played in the SEB colours of the time, emerald and amber.

SEB's first league match took place in September 1954 at Clayfield Copse, where they entertained Henley YMCA and were roundly beaten 12-0. That first ever line-up was: Terry Mason, John Norcott, Alec Leach, Pete Jones, Ted Wingrove, Ted Winkworth, Bert Wiltshire, Sony Saunders, Jack McKenzie, Arthur Hall and Reg Knott. In their second game they managed a rather more respectable 3-0 defeat at the hands of RAF Associates. The club's first ever win turned out to be a 6-3 victory over Peppard Sports on October 15, 1954.

By 1962 SEB had reached Division One of the Institute League and two seasons later achieved a record 18-0 victory over Hillier Sports in the Reading Challenge Cup, with Ron Reed hitting no fewer than 11 goals.

It was at this time that the club began running a reserve section and also moved their headquarters from Clayfield Copse to Christchurch Meadows, where they still play today.

By the late 1960s the club had begun annual tours to Europe and over a period of five seasons visited teams in Belgium, Holland, Luxembourg, France and Germany. While taking a few hidings on the pitch, they were treated like international stars off it.

Nilvange fixture

In 1964 they played a team from Nilvange in Eastern France. Having marched through the town behind a brass band, they were introduced to local dignitaries including the Mayor, and the captain Dave Lewis received flowers from the local beauty queen. They were then shown the local stadium with its large tiled dressing rooms. However, within a few minutes of the game starting, it became quite apparent that the hosts were of semi-professional standard and SEB were undone by eight goals to nil, having been six down at the break.

SEB's best year came in 1994, when they won the Reading Football League Division One Thames Section and also became divisional champions by beating Division 1 Kennet winners Sutton Exiles 5-2 in a thrilling play-off final.

The club have created some unique records during their 42-year history. In 1993, in a Jubilee Cup match, a club first was created with a father and son both scoring in the same game –

Stuart White scored twice before his father Alan added a third goal.

But the strangest of incidents took place in 1964 when the club managed to field two reserve sides on the same day. In November 1964, the bad weather had led to a huge fixture backlog in the Combination League. The first team game was cancelled and the league granted SEB permission to split the first XI, so half would join with one half of the reserve side thus clearing two reserve fixtures in one day. One team lost to Maidenhead Social Reserves whilst the other beat a rather disgruntled Theale Reserve side.

The team moved to Christchurch Meadows in the early sixties but they had to wait for nearly 20 years before they had showers in the changing rooms

READING OLD BLUES

This club was officially founded in 1952 to provide football for the former pupils of the Reading Blue Coat School. The side may have been in action in the 1930s, but there is little documented history of the team, and there is a strong suggestion that the club was moved from the league. In 1952 Len Siney became president of the Old Blues Association and decided to form a football section. He religiously prepared reports and minutes for meetings and for the 30-odd vice-presidents of the association, on the progress of the club. He also kept records of match statistics to a degree verging on the obsessional. If any of the local papers reported any of the Old Blues Statistics incorrectly, Len would spot it and be on to them like a shot.

The club have never actually played at the school. Their first pitch was on the Adwest ground, which was shared with Berkshire County Sports. For a while they played at Palmer Park, and then moved back to Adwest. They were forced to move in 1973 when Berkshire County Sports began a reserve side. The Old Blues eventually settled at Sol Joel's.

Most of the current First XI are former pupils but the club have found it necessary to relax the ruling that used to preclude anyone other than Blue Coat Old Boys from playing. The club enjoy an excellent loyalty record with players remaining with them throughout their entire playing years.

Harold Prismall became captain of the Old Blues in 1956 and played for them for nine seasons, clocking up over 200 goals in 265 appearances.

Dave Johnson played 436 games between 1969 and 1991, an amazing feat given that a league season probably consists of little more than 25 games. Stuart Walker, a former club chairman, clocked up a total of 388 appearances in the First XI and Reserves, scoring 330 goals in the process, whilst his brother,

Duncan, the current chairman, managed 422 appearances.

Bob Few is still playing and has now turned out for more than 400 games, while Clive Lovett and Luke Harris have both exceeded the 300 mark.

The First XI's only cup final appearance came in the Berkshire Trophy Centre cup of 1989-90, in which they were defeated 4-1 at the hands of Apollo.

READING YMCA

Founded in 1897, the club originally competed as St George's, the name of the boys' club to which the players were affiliated. By the early 1940s the side had changed its name from Mount Pleasant, where this particular branch of the YMCA was situated, to Reading YMCA. As a Young Men's Christian Association, the club at first objected to football being played on a Sunday, but they now run an under-14 side on that day whilst the senior side continues to play on Saturdays.

Like many clubs YMCA enjoyed its best spell in the 1950s. They originally played at Kings Meadow and used the Old Swimming Pool as a changing room which, by all accounts, stank! There were no showers or lighting and eventually the decision was taken to change at the YMCA headquarters in Friar Street and the players would all walk to the pitch. From here the club moved on to play at Christchurch Meadows and the Palmer Park track, which they shared with East Reading Adult School and finally to Coley rec where they now play.

The leading light within the club has undoubtedly been Wilf Fewtrell who has been involved with the boys' club for 53 years, initially as a player, and now as a youth leader. During his playing days, Wilf can recall riding around town on his bike checking the availability of players for the weekend match. Back in the 50s players had to take public transport to away matches at places like Sandhurst and Newbury. There was a communal bike ride to other away matches that were not so far afield.

Another star of this period was former YMCA player Bill Pearcy who, it is said, was curling the ball before the Italians and Spaniards had even dreamed of it. Bill, who played for Reading reserves during the war, joined YMCA from Windsor and Eton and became YM's captain.

Back in the late 1940s, Ted Drake, then Reading manager, used to attend presentation evenings at the boys' club and insisted that all the young Reading players were affiliated to the YMCA, so he knew where they would be in the evenings.

Wilf Fewtrell has fond memories of his days as a player and recalls many of the characters from that time. He can remember one occasion when top referee Lionel Gibbs was down at Kings Meadow changing under a tree, in readiness to officiate a YMCA game. The players were in awe – the week before Mr Gibbs had taken charge of a match at Chelsea in front of 60,000 people

44

Wilf has for some years now been involved with the running of the Berkshire Boys' Clubs' representative team. Each year he and a group of selectors hold a trial match at Prospect Park in which lads from the various boys' clubs around the county compete for a place in the under-16 representative team. If selected they get to compete in the Gillette Cup, a national boys' clubs competition. Three years ago Berkshire were just one game from Wembley when they lost their Southern area semi-final against Hertfordshire.

CAVALIERS

Roy Budd, vice-president of the Sunday league, has been the secretary of Cavaliers Football Club for 25 years. He explains how the club was established:

'The Sunday league started in 1964. Twenty-five years ago the kids in Coley asked me to try and get them into the Sunday league youth league and that's how Cavaliers started. In 1970 we were affiliated. My son was one of them - he's 37 now, he was 12 then. Before that they didn't have anywhere to play, and we had to go to Purley every Sunday to play our first matches. They wanted to start their own team and they roped me in to help them. I'm still at it.

'We were originally called Heron Youth, because we live at Heron Way, but when we went into the senior league in 1974, we had to change our name because there was a team called Heron already. The local pub was called the Roundhead so we became Cavaliers.'

The club was founded in 1970 and went into the under-13 and under-15 youth leagues where they spent four seasons. They then joined the Sunday League, going into Division Six. They came fourth in their first season and quickly progressed to the Premier League. Cavaliers have reached the final of the Ted Cambridge Cup, and won the Premier League. In the 1991-1992 season they won the Premier Division and now compete in Reading Senior Division.

Over the years Roy has had to face the growing financial difficulties of running a local club:

'Twenty-five years is a long time and there's a very different attitude now. It is a lot harder. It's got very, very expensive. The pitch at Coley rec is close on £39 a week. Referees cost £11. If I've got two teams up there of a Sunday morning I'm looking for £100. We run a pontoon, we try to do race nights, we run bus stops, we just scrounge, that's the truth of it. Team members pay £3.50 if they play - if they don't play they don't pay. That's quite cheap - some clubs would charge them £5. When we started it was half a crown a week, 12-and-a-half-pence. That

Cavaliers grew from humble origins. Roy Budd recalls: 'When we played at Purley, Mrs Diane Silman was my treasurer, and her husband used to make two trips to take the players out and then come back for me. There was only one car.'

'With youth football, mums and dads will pay their sons' subs. It keeps the kids off the street.'
Roy Budd

was youth football. We've been as low as a £1 a week subs and got by but there's no way you could do that now.'

Roy runs a tight club and believes in discipline.

'We've always been a strict club - I think it's very good for their discipline at youth level. I have to go by the rules so they go by our rules. They let their steam out on the pitch and they should have let it out on the street. Frustration comes out when they are playing the game. They see what happens on the telly. I love football but I rarely watch it now. We've had trouble on the pitch one week with bad language and I've told them, "Cut it out. You don't know who's walking round that pitch." I'm no prude. A good referee, if it's a one off, he'll let it go. But you can't let it go all the way through the game.

'Do you know what I think killed local football? The two Ss – substitutes and sponsorship. I mean that. Clubs get a sponsor and they think they're in clover but when that sponsor walks away they're in muck. Advance Windows sponsor us but the only thing they give us is kit. Clubs advertise for sponsorship now. I wouldn't lower myself. Our sponsors are the clientele of the Roundhead. We are very lucky with them, they are generous people. The pontoon they run has bought us in £600 this year.

'Football's part of life for me and it's always been a football crazy town. I think sport has got to be in your blood. I've enjoyed the Cavaliers but it's not like it used to be. I've got older and I find it harder. It's only natural. People say, "You'll never pack it in. What would you do?" I could go and watch a game of football anywhere.

'The biggest disappointment that I have experienced was that a fortnight before we went on a trip to Ireland I had my heart attack and couldn't go. That was the only tour I ever arranged. They had a wonderful time but I wasn't with them.'

READING TOWN FC

Reading Town FC, Reading's senior amateur club, was formed in 1966 but underwent various name changes in the first years of its life. Now based at Scours Lane, it has risen through the leagues – Reading Combination, Reading and District, Chiltonian League – and was newly-promoted to the Combined Counties League in the 1995-6 season. Roland 'Roly' Ford talks about its history:

'Originally Reading Town started its life as XL United, not to be confused with Exiles. XL United was a team that played at Lower Burghfield and the story goes that the farmer's son who played for the team got dropped and when that happened the team had to move to Whitley. That's when I got involved with them.

46

'We had several seasons as XL and then, in 1972, we became the first local team to get sponsored. Our sponsors were Vincents Cars, which was later bought by Reading Garage. We were very successful as Reading Garage and won everything, including the Town Cup.

'Over the next five or six years we changed our name twice. Because we wanted to keep the sponsorship, which was an important part of our development, we decided to call ourselves Reading Town and add the name of any sponsor we got. A company called ITS sponsored us so we were then called ITS Reading Town. When ITS stopped their sponsorship, we just reverted to Reading Town.

'In the meantime we had gone from the Reading Combination Football League, where we were very successful, into the Reading District League where we became runners-up two years running.

'We were movers to try to get the Reading League to create a senior division and some of the people involved still think that was a good idea. Two years after that, the Charrington Chiltonian League rose from the ashes and took the top seven sides in Reading including us.

'I regretted that because I always felt that Reading should have a senior league. In the early days there was no better football than Reading League, but unfortunately, as with most sports, the attitude towards football by the people who play it could be improved.

'Now we have the situation where if you don't pick the players up and drop them off they don't play. The attitude has changed totally. In those days there were some great characters and it was a tremendous sport for socialising. There are not those sort of characters any more and that's why I miss Reading League. I put a lot into it but I also got an immeasurable amount of pleasure out of it.

'I got involved in the management side quite early on when a knee injury stopped me playing. When I was about 23 I managed a bunch of lads from the Railway and we ended up winning the League that year. But when we went to pick our medals up, some of them had a few drinks, they started fighting and I just couldn't handle it. I thought, "That's not what football's all about", so I packed up. Then I had a phone call from XL United inviting me to join them and I did. Gil Burgess was the guy who was running things, and we bought one or two butterflies in and we kept adding to the squad until we started going up.

'What we believe down here is that Reading deserves to have a senior amateur side. That's where we see ourselves. You've got Wokingham, Newbury, Thatcham. There's some superb boys who go down to the Isle of Wight to play every week. They go to places like Staines and Marlow, because they're paid more - £10 or an extra £20 to play.

'I used to go out on a Sunday and watch the games and pick players up. I was always on the phone. Whenever you saw me I had a book in my hand trying to sign somebody. I was renowned for it. Everyone used to say. "Here's bloody Roly Ford - signing everybody in the town." But people should have been flattered if I tried to sign them because it meant I thought they were good.'
Roland Ford

In 1993-94 , the first and reserve teams of Reading Town, newly located to Scours Lane, both reached the finals of the Reading Senior and Junior Challenge Cups respectively with the reserves ending runners-up in their league. The following season Reading Town became champions of the Chiltonian Premier League, winning 21 out of 24 games. Reserves were runners-up in their league again

'We don't get many people down here really but we have had 300 or so when we've had a good local derby. On average we probably get 25 to 40 people watching but we are expecting a lot more this year. We're getting the place together and spending lots of money, like having tarmac put down. We need a great deal of money. We do fundraising and we raise money from over the bar.'

Roland Ford

There's no senior alternative in Reading. Now that we're becoming that senior alternative, we hope to get them down here.

'In the Combined Counties League, there's a mix of teams - some pay expenses, some pay the players and some don't pay anything. We just pay travelling and expenses. There are some teams that pay £50 or £60 to players. The next step is the Icis League, the former Isthmian League, which is semi-professional.

'It was great to win this League last year but I think that possibly my proudest memory was when we won the Reading Senior Cup at Elm Park. We made it a big day out. It was also nice to get recognition as the Chronicle's Manager of the Year and I've managed all the rep sides in the district combo – that was great, because you're working with class players. I've had many lovely memories really.'

Mick Price has been connected with Reading Town for about 10 years. He has been manager, assistant manager, manager of reserves and physio. He clearly remembers his first game for Reading Town:

'When I first came to Reading I was playing for Tilehurst, which was the top team when I first came, and then Roland mentioned his team which were playing on Saturdays. Well, I went over and had a look and I liked the set-up so I said I would come over and join them. I was then invited to take the Reserves on Saturday although I didn't know a

Reading Town has been busy developing its youth policy over the last two years and about 60 boys play in the five teams. The under-9s are in the Reading Friendly League and the under 10s (the 1994-5 team is pictured above), under-11s and 12s play in the South Chiltern Minor League. There is also an under-14 team.

soul. I was asked to join them at Shepherd's Hill roundabout and there were about six cars. I got out of mine and said, "Hello, lads, I'm Micky Price."

'They looked at me a bit oddly as I had come straight from work and I hadn't had time to change – I was a milkman at that time.

'We were playing at Broadmoor and we had a bare 11 players. One of the players got injured and they said, "You'll have to fill in." I hadn't got a thing with me, not even a towel, so I borrowed a pair of boots. I had got my long johns on and there were muffled comments when I took my trousers off.

'I went in for the second half and we drew one-all. I got blamed for the goal although someone over the other side of the pitch had scored. I got blamed for everything. Then we went into the dressing rooms and I hadn't got a towel, but I thought, well I've got my long johns and thermal vest so I'll dry myself on those. So I borrowed a bit of soap and went and had a shower. When I came out I went to get the long johns and vest and found they had gone. Then I hear a voice say, "Is this what you're looking for?" What they had done was lay the long johns out on the bottom of the showers so they wouldn't get their feet dirty. They had gone from about five foot to seven foot and they were covered in dirt. That was my introduction to Reading Town Football Club, and over the years it got worse.'

WEST READING

West Reading was formed in 1928 and had a largely undistinguished career in the Reading and District League before the Second World War. The club's activities were suspended for the duration of the war, but in 1946 the League restarted. West Reading received an influx of new enthusiasts when Vic Beasley and Tom Raven took over its organisation. During the late 40s and early 50s it was 'just plodding along in the Premier Division' as current chairman Jack Jarvis remembers.

West Reading won the Premier division in 1956, and won the league in the 1961-62 season, but the team's 'Glory Years' did not begin until the early 60s. They won the Berks and Bucks Intermediate Cups in 1964-65, 1966- 67, 1968-69, and 1971-72. (Whichever team won the Intermediate Cup entered

'Once I hit a bloke over the head with my water bucket because he'd kicked one of the players. I tried saying that the guy had slipped and head-butted my bucket but it didn't work.'

Mick Price

West Reading FC 1967 (back row): Tony Lawrence, Pete Bartlett, Dave Chard (captain), Gordon Smith, Tony Bampton, Mick Wells. Front row: Gordon Richards (trainer), Eric Richardson, Dave Burbedge, Terry Bampton, Dave Bunch, Jack Jarvis.

Jack Jarvis recalls Tom Raven – the man who was 'Mr West Reading'. 'He was the most respected man, the most respected manager. He never gave anybody any praise, he just moaned and groaned, but we all loved him.'

Tom Raven (centre) with Dave Chard and Dave Burbedge after winning the Berks and Bucks Intermediate Cup Final in 1984

'I don't think it's the same today but in those days you were very, very committed to the team. All the lads will tell you that we lived for Saturday afternoons. You will find that when we were youngsters we hardly went to a family wedding.'

Peter Bartlett

for the Senior Cup the next year, and could not then compete for the Intermediate Cup until the following year.)

West Reading also had a very strong reserves team, and won Division One three times from 1959 to 1965. Jack Jarvis comments:

'The reserves were so successful they were a little bit reluctant when they got selected for the first team; they wanted to stay in the reserves. The reserves were having such a wonderful season and they had this great camaraderie and they really didn't want to leave their mates and come in the first team.'

West Reading now play at Victoria rec in Tilehurst, but during this period they played on the pitch just below the bowling green at Prospect Park. Terry Bampton, a former player, recalls:

'It was as big as Elm Park but most of the rivals didn't like it and thought it was a rubbish pitch. It was a bit undulating but we liked it, we thought it was a very good pitch.'

At one time there was discussion about West Reading trying to enter a higher league. The chairman of the time, Vic Beasley, was keen on the idea, but Tom Raven did not want the club to leave the Reading and District League. There was also the issue of pitches. Tony Bampton explains:

'The reason West Reading didn't go for the higher league, and lots of people used to say to me we ought to, was that we didn't have our own ground. If we could have had somewhere like Huntley and Palmers or Courage, we could have possibly got to the Spartan League.'

Tony Bampton recalls West Reading's best games:

'I reckon that West Reading played the most important game that's ever been played in local park fooball in Reading, and that was when we played Chesham United in the quarter final of the Berks and Bucks Senior Cup. If we'd beaten them, and we had a reasonable chance, we could have played Wycombe Wanderers' first team in the semi-final. Well, we were in the quarter-final and I would say, purely as park team that was the most important game ever played in Reading.'

Terry Bampton remembers another highlight:

'The best game over the years was the game before that. We played Aylesbury, who were a big strong side, at Huntley and Palmers. We were only a park team even though we were quite a good side and we beat them 3-2.'

There was a strong and still-remembered rivalry between West Reading and Rabsons. However, players of the time say that any hostility between the sides took place only on the pitch and was immediately forgotten. Jack Jarvis recalls:

'Off the field we loved each other but on the field there was this tremendous Rabsons/West Reading thing. Every time we played there was a big crowd. Every year, all through the season, one of us was second and one of was first. We used to end up at the Olympia on London Street on a Saturday night giving each other stick. It was a wonderful thing, it really was. I've not seen it since. I think perhaps now there'd be a punch-up.'

But the glory days came to an end as Jack Jarvis remembers:

'I took over as manager in 1978 when Tom Raven passed on. I honestly could see it was the end of an era because the Bunches, the Burbedges, the twins, were all into their 30s. I knew then that within three years West Reading would become an ordinary side again. All these players began to get old together. We won the league, we won the Reading Senior Cup, but we certainly weren't going like we were before. It wasn't anybody's fault. The younger generation came in, with discos, the all-night raves, Sky television, and Sunday football became a big thing.'

RABSON ROVERS

Rabson Rovers, which celebrated its 50th anniversary on May 23, 1992, was originally formed as a friendly side in 1941 known as Whitley Swifts, but it wasn't until 1942 that they were established, changing their names to Rabson Rovers when they moved to Rabsons rereation ground. The main founders of the club were Harold Prosser, Maurice Honor, Doug Cordery and Harry Hawkins, with Doug Bryan as secretary. They started the club to play friendlies while several of the team members were waiting to be called up.

After the war the team entered the Reading and District League. Dick Bennett and his committee took over in 1952 and it became one of the most successful local clubs.

They were the first Reading football club to win the Berks and Bucks Intermediate Cup on April 16, 1960. Their most successful seasons were 1963-4, when they won the Berks and Bucks Intermediate Cup and Reading Senior Challenge Cup, and 1964-5, when they won the Premier Division, Reading and District League; Division One, section B, Reading and District League; and Reading Senior Challenge Cup.

Bob Bennett, son of Dick Bennett and life vice-president of Rabsons, reminisces with his wife Trish, his mother Joan Bennett, and former Rabsons stalwarts Ray 'Sam' Maynard and Jack Ingram.

Jack: The first cup final we ever played was 1948 against Cholsey. We got beaten 1-0. I was in the reserves.

Rabsons was in danger of folding when Dickie Bennett took it over. He was a big man with a big heart. 'It was Dickie who made the club. He was the nub. He pulled it all together. He was Rabsons, there was no doubt about that, he was a great bloke. He'd help anybody. If he wanted a job doing, he'd do it.'

Sam Maynard

'When I was 14 or 15 I got paid for scoring goals. It was an inducement to put the ball in the back of the net. I got a shilling a goal. That was a lot of money. If you got a hat trick you were laughing, you got three shillings in your pocket.'

Jack Ingram

Sam: Do you remember when Mossy Alum broke the bar at Cholsey with that header? There was a great big black muddy puddle in front of the goal. It must have been in the late 60s. He was playing centre forward at the time. The ball came back off an upright and Mossy went for it and headed it and before he landed in this puddle the ball had hit the cross bar and broke it.

Jack: The changing rooms were a long cow shed, and there was a big bungalow bath.

Sam: We had to shoo the cows off the pitch before we could play.

Jack: They filled up this big bungalow bath with hot water and you jumped in and jumped out straight away.

Joan: There was a piece of wood missing from the shed and all you could see were the boys' bare bottoms.

Sam: We were playing the semi-final cup match at High Wycombe

Jack: They said 'It's a waste of time you coming here, keep the coach running'. Stratfield drove the coach – he had this big klaxon horn. That was some game.

Sam: They went off with their tails between their legs. With us, we celebrated defeats as well as victories. We would never be demoralised by getting beat. That's the sort of club we were.

Jack: At Rabsons we always went back to the club and had a cup of tea.

Sam: There was no licence so we had pints of milk. It was just a canteen. We had food laid on there – cheese rolls, my favourite bread pudding.

Jack: We used to chatter about what we were going to do to the next opposition. Six o'clock everybody stopped work and they went along for a celebration.

Sam: We trained once a week on Thursday nights and and we were down the park Sunday mornings for two or three hours even in the snow in the winter.

Trish: They wanted to be fit enough to make sure their names were there on that board on Monday night. Now you have to beg them to play. That was the difference. They wanted to play then.

Sam: There wasn't be any bad rivalry between ourselves or anybody else but we were very competitive. Many an accident happened.

Joan: I remember Lal Durden broke his leg and they took him home and put him on his doorstep and left him there. They all disappeared.

Bob: It was even competitive in the gym. Do you remember the wooden climbing wall bars, the old PE equipment with the long benches on hooks? They used take them down and lay them round the bottom so it would keep them away from the wall bars, but they used to go and kick the benches.

Sam: I can remember Lal Durden kicking the bench once – he did scream. It was an accident. He wasgoing for the ball. That's how competitive it was.

'We were playing at Cholsey and I went up to a high ball with my boot and this bloke, Frank Lake, who was playing for us, went down for it. I came up with my foot and he came down with his head and I took the top of his nose right off. So Dickie put it in a handkerchief, and took him to the cottage hospital, and they stitched it back on and we picked him up afterwards.'

Sam Maynard

Jack: We weren't any tougher than they are today but we used to play in a sporting manner.

Jack Ingram also recalls some of Rabsons' most memorable games:

'I think one of Rabsons' finest games was when we played Otley United in the semi-final of the Berks and Bucks Cup. They were top dogs in their league, they were a brilliant side. We expected to go down there and get a good hiding but we always seemed to perform against a good side like that . And once we kicked off that was it, we never looked back. The score was 3-2 to us.

'Another good game I remember was a semi-final for the Berks and Bucks Cup when we played at that waterlogged ground out at Bracknell. There was freezing water all over the ground. We never bothered to get changed. The referee came up and said. "What's up with you boys then?" We said, "We're not playing on this." But he told us: "I'll say whether you're going to play or not."'

Many people agree that Rabson was a special club because of the community spirit involved. Sam Maynard comments:

'Rabsons' people are luckier than most because we had a club where everybody got on well together and it was a homely sort of club. With Dickie and his missus and Harold and George Hawkins, you couldn't help but enjoy it. It was just like another family.'

Unfortunately, since Dick Bennett died, relations with the personnel of South Reading Community Centre declined, and many of the people involved with the club feel that this has had a detrimental effect on their football. They also feel that there is a lack of new people willing to give their time to support the club's activities.

'We got maried on September 19, 1981, and the first thing Bob had to do at the reception was phone down to see how Rabsons got on.'
Trish Bennett

They all had nom de plumes - Thatcher Wheeler, Razor Smith, Toff Warwick, Jacko Shepherd, Taff Butler, Badger Smith, Chopper Hughes, Offside Ingram, Jim Lad Hawkins.

Rabson Rovers line-up during their glory days

*A group of Rabson Rovers'
loyal supporters*

However Bob and Trish Bennett are still deeply involved. It's in the Bennett blood. Trish recalls how one day her 11-year-old son Alastair, grandson of Dickie Bennett, said to his father: "When you die, Daddy, will Rabsons be mine?" She added: 'It's a family to our kids, it's Rabsons.'

MORTIMER

Along with Theale, Mortimer has become one of the hotbeds of local football, with several different sides emerging from the village over the years. A Mortimer club was in existence prior to the First World War, playing in the Reading Wednesday League. By the 1920s 'The Garth' had become established as the village's premier outfit. The side was an extension of the youth club of the same name formed by Miss Capron. In later years the top side became Mortimer Men's Club FC and another village side, nicknamed 'The City,' were also strong during the 1950s. In 1985, The Garth and The Men's club merged to form Mortimer FC as it exists today. The newly-formed club was to cater for both Saturday and Sunday football.

The club currently operates with first and reserve teams on both days. The Mortimer Saturday side have in recent seasons become Reading's most successful side. In 1992-93 they were runners-up in the Reading Evening Post Senior Cup. This near miss was followed by two successive senior division titles and season 1993-94 saw the club's greatest achievement when they became one of just a handful of Reading clubs to have captured the Berks and Bucks Intermediate Cup.

PARK LANE (SUNDAY)

Formed in 1957, Park Lane have only played under their current name since 1993. The club was originally the Heelas works side, but the company eventually withdrew financial support when it became clear that the club was not being run for the benefit of their own staff and 'outsiders' were coming to play for the club. Consequently the team went in search of a financial backer and received the support of Masterplan financial services. However the club couldn't take the company name as its own as again few of the workforce actually played for the club. The decision was taken to use the name Park Lane, where the firm's Tilehurst office is situated.

IBIS

Although by no means one of the older clubs in the town, Ibis are by far the biggest, with four teams currently in existence on Saturdays and three more on Sundays. There is some debate over the origin of the club name. A sports and social club of the Prudential Assurance Company had been in existence in London for some time when, in the 1870s, a Mr T H Richardson is said to have proposed a short and distinctive name for the club and came up with the name Ibis.

A rather more credible theory and the one that is now widely recognised at the club is that the company used to be split into two separate operations; the Industrial and Ordinary branches. The two used to compete against each other in all manner of activities and the Industrial Branch teams were encouraged with cries of, 'Come on IBs'. The name stuck and when Prudential moved part of its operation to Reading, the new sports facilities at Scours Lane effectively became an extension of the London Ibis club at Chiswick.

The Reading Ibis Football Club (Saturdays) was founded in 1964 and before the current clubhouse was constructed the players used to change at the Pond House pub on the Oxford Road before walking down to the Scours Lane pitch. In 1965-66 a marquee was erected and used as a changing facility until the club house was completed later in 1964.

Although the club in Reading was formed in the same year as the Reading Sunday League, they were not amongst the early competitors in that league and a Sunday side wasn't formed until the 1972-73 season.

THE ROYAL BERKSHIRE REGIMENT

One team which is no longer in existence was virtually invincible in its day. The 4/6th Battalion, The Royal Berkshire Regiment (Territorial Army), based at Brock Barracks in Oxford Road, Reading, boasted a football team filled with players from senior amateur football. On several occasions the side won the National TA Cup, beating sides from all over the country, and when the Reading Sunday League began in 1964, Royal Berks (TA) were the senior section champions for the first two seasons. With the impending reorganisation of the TA in the mid-1960s, the team folded, but not before its greatest ever triumph.

As TA Cup winners for 1965-66, Royal Berks met the Regular Army Cup winners, 24th Signal Regiment, in a play-off at Huntley and Palmers FC ground, Kensington Road, on

There are differing opinions on how IBIS got its name, though it seems to have come from the fans shouting to the Industrial Branch Team, 'Come on IBs.'

October 2, 1966. The local part-time soldiers won the game 3-2, with goals from Ken Lunnon, Jimmy Messer and Terry Warth, though the decisive moment of the game came when goalkeeper Derek Sparkes saved a penalty kick with the scores level at 2-2. A unique feature of the game was that it was controlled, as an experiment, by two referees, rather than a referee and two linesmen.

THE MAIWAND LIONS

The cream of local football was represented abroad for a few short years, between 1975 and 1980, by a touring squad called the Maiwand Lions. The object was to play hard – in both senses – and the team made a lasting impression.

In the mid-70s a group of key people from the Saturday and Sunday Leagues got together to create a side to travel abroad each season. They included Chippy Taylor, Ted Cambridge, Gordon Bartlett, Paul Hopes, Andy Bryan, Dick Leach, Charlie Strong, Roland Ford, Jack Jarvis, Leon Summer, George Leach, Alan Finch, Albie Cohen, Eric Munt, Peter Russell, Bill Brown-Lee, and Roy Murdoch. They called themselves the Maiwand Lions after the Forbury Gardens lion.

Between 1975 and 1980 a team representing local footballers formed a touring squad which visited Europe and America. 'It was a sad thing that the recession came and we were never able to pick it all up again. We're still trying to get it resurrected.'

Roy Murdoch

Their first game was held, rather sooner than planned, at the end of August 1975 in Reading against a team from George Washington University. A football coach from the university, a Haitian International, had contacted Roy Murdoch out of the blue asking for help with a British tour:

'We quickly selected a group of all the well-known players of the area at the time, Dave Chard, Dave Burbedge, Roger Harris, Charlie Palmer, Mo Palmer, Keith James, and the like, and we arranged for the game to be played down at what was the old Heelas ground, then a very nice facility, which was later taken over by Reading Town.

'The Mayor of Reading kicked off for us, we had a very good crowd, and we were successful. But more importantly we made good friends with this touring group, so much so that they asked us to go over to America and play them the following year.'

So in 1976 group of about 30 including a 16-player squad went to the USA, played eight games in the Washington DC area and finished off with a holiday in Florida. They had such a successful time that they were asked back the following year. This time they spent one week in North Carolina, one week in South Carolina, and five days' holiday in the Bahamas.

The trips were heavily subsidised for the 16 players chosen to go on the tours and the extra funds were raised by the Lions at raffles, horseracing nights, dances, and other events.

In 1978, Maiwand decided to send two youth teams instead of a men's team. An under-14 side visited Williamsburg, Washington DC and Maryland, and Roy recalls:

'There were 16 teams in our section, and we won every game. I think we had one goal scored against us in the whole tournament, and we were absolutely superb. The crowds there loved the way we played and loved the way our boys conducted themselves. Several of the team signed for pro teams later but none of them made big names.'

In the autumn Maiwand sent over an under-15 team, which included Neil Webb, to play in Pennsylvania. Again the team enjoyed considerable success, and after they played in Reading, Berkshire, Pennsylvania, they were made honorary citizens of the town. An under-23 team also toured Holland and Germany.

In 1979 Maiwand Lions visited San Diego, San Francisco, and Mexico, and were again unbeaten in eight games. 'But the main thing was the good friendships that were forged everywhere,' said Roy.

The last tour that the Maiwand Lions arranged took place in 1980 when the squad returned to San Diego and Mexico. But by now the UK was just going into a recession, and it was becoming increasingly difficult to obtain the sponsorship necessary for the players to travel abroad. The tours abroad, and the reciprocal visits to Reading by teams from America and Europe, came to an end.

The Maiwand Lions still exist as an entity, but they never really recovered from the recession of the early 1980s. However, the club did forge international friendships which are remembered to this day. 'We still get-together,' says Roy. 'Wonderful times were had by so many.'

On the second tour, the boys invented a gag called 'dead rats'. One member of the touring team was nominated as caller for the day, and whenever he shouted 'dead rats', everyone else had to dive down, lie on their backs and waggle their legs in the air, like dying rats. Whoever was last down had to pay for a round of drinks or put some money into a kitty for the last night's celebration.

THE PARK SOCCER SCENE IN READING
by Clive Baskerville, Reading Evening Post

When the Post first started reporting on park soccer in Reading, Dave Chard was a tiger-tackling defender, Dave Burbedge was a young thoroughbred with an astute eye for goal, Ray Ball and Jack Jarvis were nippy wingers, Dave Jeanes was approaching his prime, Dave Bunch, Cliff Tuttle and Peter Bartlett were outwitting opponents week after week, and the Bampton twins were confusing referees.

They were the good old days, my colleagues tell me. There are many arguments as whether it is better now than it was, say, 20 years ago. Perhaps there are not so many characters playing these days, but the current crop look younger and fitter. There are also a lot more players about.

Once there were two Saturday leagues, the District and the Combination, and now there is one, the Reading Football League. One of their priorities has been to improve the standard of football and they have definitely succeeded. The Reading Sunday League has grown and grown, and the general opinion is that the standard in the top divisions has never been higher.

All these teams, of course, need somewhere to play and Reading Borough Council have had to mow and mark out many new pitches to accommodate them. All the groundsmen deserve credit for keeping them playable up until Spring of each year.

Over the years, it is youth soccer that has developed the most. There cannot be many parts of Reading which are not represented by at least one youth team. Girls and ladies' football has also taken off in a big way and new teams are being formed each year.

Boys start at a very young age and I do have my doubts about whether they are too young to be kicking a ball in anger. I feel they should be concentrating more on learning the basic skills at this age rather than trying to win league titles and cups. I believe it would be better if no boy, or girl, was allowed to play a competitive game until the age of 10 or even 12.

Reading has been crying out for a senior non-league club for many years. We used to have Huntley and Palmers playing in the Spartan League, making them the second most important club in the town to Football Leaguers Reading. Peppard, who have several players living in the Reading area, have enjoyed success in the Combined Counties League but now we have a club right in the heart of the town who are challenging them as the top non-league club in the area.

Reading Town are part of the soccer pyramid, which allows clubs like them to climb up the ladder and go via the Icis League into the Conference League, just one step outside the Endsleigh Insurance Football League. I'm not suggesting that we will see Reading Town reach these dizzy heights but the pyramid at least gives ambitious clubs like them an incentive to build up their resources brick by brick. Watch their progress!

4 Local Heroes

Internationals and Personality Players

READING'S INTERNATIONALS

by Bryan Horsnell

A town the size of Reading cannot expect to compete alongside the major cities of London, Birmingham, Liverpool or Manchester when it comes to personality players. Nevertheless, several Reading-born or based players have secured their own niche in football history as international players, from schoolboy right up to full international level.

SCHOOLBOY INTERNATIONALS

Twelve-year-old Leonard Grant was a Schoolboy International who spent his formative years at Battle School in Kensington Road, Reading, in the late 1890s and early 1900s. The English Schools Football Association was founded in 1904, but it was not until 1907 that the idea of a Schoolboy International was first mooted by the committee of the time. The Scottish and Irish Schools Football Associations had not yet been founded, so it was suggested that a match should be arranged between an England Schools' team and one from schools in Wales, to be played at Walsall's Hillary Street Ground on April 13, 1907.

The England team in that historic first Schoolboy International of almost 90 years ago included young Leonard Grant from Battle School, Reading. When I met Len Grant he was 74 years old but still vividly remembered his big day in 1907, the events that preceded his appearance for the England Boys, and his subsequent football career.

Len commented:

'When I got into the Reading Boys team in 1906 I was only 11 years old, but we had a very good side and we managed to reach the semi-finals of the English Schools' Shield. We beat Croydon, Brentford, Watford and Walsall and then had to travel up to Sunderland for the semi-final. I had never been far out of Reading and it seemed like another world travelling all the way up to the north-east of England.

'The match, against the Sunderland Boys, was played at Roker Park in front of a crowd of 15,000. It was a good game and they beat us 3-0, but I must have done all right as a little while after I heard that I had been picked for the England team. At the time, I didn't have any proper

Schoolboy internationals are now an accepted part of the football calendar and the present England Boys Under-15 team regularly plays half a dozen or so internationals against the likes of Brazil, Germany, Holland, France, as well as the 'home' countries, Scotland, Ireland and Wales, every season.

Len Grant as a boy

The Reading Schools' FA were so proud of their local boy's achievement that they asked Len Grant to turn out for Reading Boys in a match at Elm Park wearing his international cap! It was a cold wet afternoon and the addition of the precious piece of headgear proved quite a handicap as he was loath to head the ball when it came his way

football boots. I used to play in the boots I wore every day to school, but the Reading Schools Football Association bought me a pair for the match against Wales, at Walsall. I usually played at full-back, but I was picked to play at left-half for England and we beat the Welsh boys 3-1.'

Nowadays, almost every England Schoolboy International is already on the books of a Football League or Premiership club and, almost without exception, most of them have the opportunity to become a professional footballer. This wasn't the case back in 1907. Upon leaving school, Len Grant joined the local firm of G R Jackson, but continued with his football and later became a regular member of the crack local amateur side Reading United. Len also turned out for Reading Reserves on numerous occasions, as an amateur, and in 1921 he signed professional forms for the club.

Len recalled:

'My wages were £3 a week, during the season and 30 shillings (£1.50) during the summer. Even at the end of my professional playing career in 1925 when I was a first team regular and captain of the club I was only drawing £5 winter and £3 summer weekly wages.'

After making his Football League debut for Reading in October 1921, Len became the regular right-back for the remainder of the season, making a total of 33 appearances. In the 1923-24 season he captained the side to a 2-1 win over Brighton in the annual Royal Berkshire Hospital Charity Cup match, at Elm Park.

His consistent and polished displays were attracting the attention of many of the big London clubs, but Len had no desire to leave the town where he had spent all his life.

Len Grant

He was plagued by a recurring leg injury, and in the summer of 1925 he decided to hang up his boots and continue to work for Jackson's. He remained there until ill health forced him to retire, at the age of 73, after almost 60 years with the firm. Len Grant died on March 19, 1967.

YOUTH FOOTBALL

Reading's first youth international Ray Reeves made his England debut against Wales on February 26, 1949, at Swansea's Vetch Field ground, before a then record youth international crowd of 52,000

It wasn't until 1948 that England fielded their first Youth International team.

In 1949 Reading's Raymond Reeves, a young left-back was selected for the 1949 England Youth squad, following some outstanding displays for the Berks and Bucks FA Youth XI in the County Youth Championship. Ray made his debut in February 1949, and in April 1949 was a member of the England squad which took part in an International Youth

Adrian Williams
Profile by Clive Baskerville

Adrian was first introduced to Reading FC by one of his predecessors at Elm Park, Steve Wood, who played centre-back for Royals from 1980-87, and coached a boys' team in Bracknell called Clark-Eaton, later Bracknell Boys' Club.

Four of the boys from that team were introduced to Reading's Centre of Excellence, a scheme to develop the best local talent in the area, in 1982 when Adrian was 11. The other lads were Scott Taylor, Steve Holzman and Ryan Cleverly.

Williams' early career received a boost when he moved to Wokingham Town to play for their junior sides. He appeared in their highly successful under-13 and 14 teams, winning a batch of medals. Also in that squad were future Royals' colleague Stuart Lovell and several stars who went on to join other football league sides, like Darren Barnard (Chelsea and Bristol City), Steve Banks (Gillingham and Blackpool), Paul Wilkinson (Brighton) and Billy Seymour (Coventry). Adrian comments:

'They had an excellent set-up and we won titles in the West Surrey League. We also went on tours to places like Great Yarmouth, which gave us the feel of being involved in a team that was worth playing for. Although I played football at school, I wasn't a regular in the East Berks representative side, unlike Scottie, but I didn't lose any sleep over it. In those days I was a skinny right winger, and I didn't go into the defence until I played for Reading.

'I owe a lot to Reading youth coach Stewart Henderson and manager Ian Branfoot because they recognised my potential as a defender and encouraged me to change. I always remember in my debut for Reading's first team as a 17-year-old, Branfoot helped talk me through the game. In the first half I was on the dug-out side, so he wasn't far away. But in the second half he took a chair over to the other side of the field so he could stay in touch. Some of the experienced players also helped me through the game and we finished up getting a draw.'

It wasn't long before Adrian scored his first goal from a set piece against Hereford in the Associate Members' Cup. His first league goal followed a few days after his 18th birthday, also from a set peice at Crewe.

'Although I don't remember too much about those games, I do recall quite a bit about our final game of the season at Chesterfield in May 1989. We had to win to stay up and I was drafted in as a right-winger. We were 2-0 down at half-time and it was very quiet in the dressing room. We were told there were only 45 minutes of our season left and

ADRIAN WILLIAMS
BORN: Royal Berks Hospital, Reading
DATE: August 16 1971
LIVES: Bracknell
SCHOOL: Meadow Vale, Bracknell; Garth Hill, Bracknell
READING DEBUT: v Notts County (A), October 1988
WALES debut: v Estonia (A), May 1994

'I'm lucky to have a father who always encouraged me but, at the same time, made me keep my feet on the floor. If I did something good, he'd pat me on the back, but if I did something wrong he'd be the first to tell me.'

Adrian Williams

'I get a real buzz out of stopping players and enjoy personal duels. Over the years you get to know the strengths and weaknesses of certain opponents and the crowd likes to see two big guys have a battle. Kevin Francis (Stockport) and Tony Philliskirk (Bolton) are two that spring to mind. No matter how many times we clashed we always seemed to get on well afterwards which is good.

'Being captain was a job I I thought I could handle and I knew I had to make my mark. Shouting instructions and encouraging players is very important, and if something needs to be said I'm not afraid to say it. It's also important to set an example off the field and conduct yourself properly. I like to think I do that well.'

Adrian Williams

that we had to go out and give it our best shot.

'We pulled a goal back through a penalty fairly quickly and went on to win 4-2. I stayed on the whole 90 minutes and the relief at the end was enormous. The way we celebrated, you'd have thought we'd just won the cup final.'

Williams' career, which had lapsed because of injury under Ian Porterfield, was restarted under Mark McGhee.

'I started off playing in centre-midfield where I was asked to win some tackles and headers. But I eventually settled into a centre-half role late in 1991 and I've never looked back.

'Since I've been picked for Wales, I've had the chance to play against some world class players, including Germany's Jurgen Klinsmann. I had a few butterflies before I faced him as a second half substitute because I wasn't sure what to expect. He never stopped running for the entire 45 minutes and he proved a difficult opponent. But we got a 1-1 draw out of the game and I enjoyed the occasion.'

Ever since he joined Reading as a YTS lad in 1987, it had been Williams' ambition to captain Royals and he achieved that goal in 1991. He became the first Reading-born skipper of the club since Jimmy Wheeler some 30 years earlier. Although barely 23 years old, Williams was already a Welsh international and had appeared in every shirt number – from 1 to 14 – for the first team.

This achievement of wearing every Reading shirt is one of which Adrian is very proud.

'When the club realised I'd played in every shirt except number 10, that was rectified when we played Wrexham in March 1994. I was due to play in midfield so I had a word with our usual number 10 (Stuart Lovell) to see if it was okay to swap. He had no objections so I created a little bit of history. I've got the picture that marked the occasion in my scrapbook and it's one I'll cherish. The achievement is a nice one and it's unusual – particularly as I managed it by the age of 22.'

Stuart and Simon Lovell
Profiles by Clive Baskerville

Although born in Australia, Caversham brothers Simon and Stuart Lovell have, between them, played through most of the different grades of football in Reading. Stuart (or Archie as he's best known to Royals fans) had a highly successful schools' record, while Simon also did well at that grade before settling into playing soccer at parks level.

Football was in the blood of the Lovells. Dad Colin played centre-forward for Ruislip Manor a generation earlier and both lads were encouraged to play. Stuart recalls:

'Although he encouraged us, he was never overpowering. He always maintained we should be two-footed because that helps you play better.'

There was fierce sibling rivalry – the boys would never play on the same side – and Stuart was always determined to put one over his older brother.

'Being younger I was always on a loser physically with Simon so I had to make up in other ways – with my wiliness and skill.'

Simon comments:

'We first played together in organised football at Micklands in six-a-side matches. I was captain of the A team but Stuart, who was two years younger, still managed to be good enough for the B side. In fact he scored eight goals in an 11-1 win against Alfred Sutton and earned promotion to the A side. Unfortunately this caused conflict between us! Stuart was teacher Mr Amiss' favourite and that didn't endear him to me. During one match, which we lost, Stuart was stood out on the wing not doing much and I had a real go at him at half time. Mr Amiss sided with Stuart saying it was disgraceful I should shout at him like that. All I remember after that was us arguing all the way home in the car.'

Stuart, after a record-breaking stint at primary schools level, was able to progress at senior school – although not always with the knowledge or consent of his teachers. He recalls:

'Although I went to school in Oxfordshire at Chiltern Edge, I was still able to play for the Reading schools' representative side. The only problem was the counties took different holiday breaks and that caused trouble for me. Reading often arranged extra games during the holidays while I was back at school across the border. The only way around it was to take time off school. I usually made an excuse that I had a dental appointment when, in fact, I was playing football at 11am. I'd get a Reading teacher to drop me off at home so I could change and then walk to the shops to get a bus to school for the afternoon.'

Stuart's prowess eventually earned him an offer of a YTS place at Reading FC when he was 16 but that didn't stop him joining in games near his home – and earning new admirers. He remembers:

'I had just left school in 1988 when I decided to try out a new pair of boots. I went up to Clayfield Copse and noticed Caversham Park training. One or two of the lads asked if I'd like to join in their shooting practice and my first four shots all went into the top corner of the net. One of the coaches said to a colleague: "Do you think he'd like to play for us?" His colleague knew me and told him I'd just signed for

STUART LOVELL

BORN: Sydney
DATE: January 9 1972
Schools: Micklands, Caversham; Chiltern Edge, Sonning Common
PLAYED: Reading Primary Schools 1981-2, 1982-3, Reading Schools U-14 and U-15, Reading FC Centre of Excellence from 1983, Wokingham Town Youth, Caversham Park Youth, Reading FC YTS 1988-90, professional 1990-today. While playing for Reading Primary he scored 57 goals which is a record tally for an individual

'I only played half a dozen games in the A team because of the way my brother shouted at me!'

Stuart Lovell

SIMON LOVELL

BORN: Sydney
DATE: November 11, 1969
SCHOOLS: Micklands,
Caversham; Chiltern Edge,
Sonning Common
PLAYED: Reading Primary
Schools 1980-81,
Caversham Park,
Rotherfield and
Wokingham Town Youth;
Caversham Park Sunday,
Courage Sunday.

'I couldn't resist watching football. Even if it was only kids kicking a tin about, I'd stop and watch them. I was always very keen on football.'

Danny Webb

Reading, which rather surprised the coach!'

That ability to surprise and impress his older colleagues continued at Elm Park, although not everyone took so kindly to being taught a lesson by a youngster. Lovell was on the receiving end of some stern advice from Mick Gooding, who had only recently joined the club from Wolves.

'The first time I joined in six-a-side games with the pros came when they were one short and needed an extra player. Coach Eddie Niedzwiecki called me over. We were playing two or three touch football and Mick was on the other side. Eventually Stuart Beavon and I found ourselves trapped in a corner and the only way out was to "nutmeg" Mick. Nutmegging is when the ball is played through a player's legs and is something pros hate done to them. In the end we both nutmegged Mick who was getting extremely annoyed.

'I had a good day and I made Mick look foolish and he responded by kicking me virtually every time I had the ball. Afterwards, Mick took me to one side and told me I'd done well but that I should never shout out "nutmeg" on the field, which apparently I'd done. I tried to explain that I thought it was the only way I was going to get the ball, but he made it clear that there's a code of practice in the game that makes that shout out of bounds. I learned a lesson that day.'

LOCAL STARS

Apart from the famous names of Reading football there are many fine local players who could have played at professional level but through choice or chance continued as amateurs, turning out fine performances season after season.

Danny Webb

One such great local player from an earlier era is Dennis 'Danny' Webb. He played for a number of local sides, including Grove Rangers, Battle Athletic, Maidenhead United and Reading Borough Police. His playing career began in 1934 and ended in 1957 when he decided to retire from the game.

Danny had an outstanding record for goalscoring, and achieved a grand total of 1,350 goals in his playing life.

In his early days Danny played for the newly-formed Battle Athletic under the tutelage of Pop Parsons and Charlie Kearse. Battle had a remarkably successful season in 1936-37. Danny recalls:

'They won all three minor trophies. That was the first time it had ever been done - the Reading Minor Cup, the Reading Minor League and the Berks/Bucks Minor Cup. And out of the 11 players who played for

that team, 11 were signed by professional clubs on amateur forms –
there used to be amateur forms in those days, and there were eight of
us signed for Reading and three for Queens Park Rangers. The outcome of it was that the team went almost en bloc to Maidenhead
United, at that time Reading's nursery team. We used to go up to Elm
Park and do our training up there on Tuesday and Thursday evenings.
Of course we used to be with all the old pros, and they used to lead us
a merry dance. There was a lot of good names up there, there was
George Marks, Tony MacPhee, and Wilf Chitty. Us boys used to chase
after those, and we had rare fun, rare fun.'

Maidenhead United won the Berks and Bucks Senior Cup in
1938, when Danny, aged 18, was one of the youngest players
ever to win a medal for his performance.

War broke out the following year and Danny was called up
in December 1939. Years in service obviously put paid to his
footballing progress, although he did play for the British Army
in Africa, Italy and in Greece, and was the only amateur in the
team.

Danny returned to England after the war and shortly after-
wards became a civilian clerk with the police. The Borough
Police football team began playing in 1949-50 in the
Wednesday League, with Danny as a member. They won the
League and the Cup that year and went on to achieve further
honours. Danny comments:

'That went on for five, six, seven years, and we swept all before us in
the Wednesday League, and there were some good teams in the
Wednesday League those days. You'd get crowds of three or four hundred up at Palmer Park track on a Wednesday afternoon, and if you
went up to Tilehurst rec you could always reckon on two or three hundred up there too, three and four deep all round the pitch. This was the
start of the resurrection of the old Wednesday League, and the Police
used to win the League and Cup nearly every year.'

Danny finished playing in 1957 at the age of 37. He left the
Police and Battle Athletic also finished as a senior side at this
time.

Danny had several remarkable skills as a footballer, not least
his superb goalscoring ability. He tries to explain his prowess:

'It wasn't till after I left school that I just got this knack of scoring goals.
I used to score goals wherever I played, whether I played in the forward line, in the halfback line or in the defence. I could play in most
positions. I loved to play centre forward, centre forward was my spot,
but they always reckoned I was a better wing half than a centre forward.

*Danny Webb had an out-
standing season in 1952-
53 when he scored a total
of 163 goals - 102 for the
Police and 61 for Battle
Athletic. On three sepa-
rate occasions he scored
10 goals in a match –
once all 10 in a row!*

*Danny Webb drawn by Syd
Jordan in 1950*

*'I used to get a kick out
of scoring goals, I used to
get a kick out of seeing
that ball in the net, you
know. And it made no
difference whether I'd
scored five or I'd scored
10.'*

Danny Webb

'We were all good friends. There was no animosity afterwards - bags of it on the pitch while it was going on, but afterwards forgotten.'

Danny Webb

The powerful Reading Borough Police team. Danny Webb is centre front

'People remember you as you were when you finished, and if you lose that little bit of speed, and you lose that little bit of timing, you become a has-been. People go past you when once upon a time they wouldn't have seen you. But that's what it is to get old! '

Danny Webb

'Up at Elm Park, they used to have a shooting gallery, about 12, 13 yards long with sloping sides and a sloping back and roof. It had a bullseye at the bottom of it, and you could hit this ball and it used to come back to you all the time, no matter how you hit it.

'I used to practise an awful lot. I think it was down to that. They used to say to me, "Oh, you get all your goals from rebounds, and rebounds off the goalkeeper's knees, and rebounds off the bar," and I said, "Well, it's just a question of being in the right place at the right time." I was always a johnny-on-the-spot, everybody caught me over 20 yards, but nobody caught me ever in the first three, and that's not easy. But as I say, 20 yards and everybody caught me. My wife could catch me!'

Danny also possessed a powerful throw. He comments:

'I had a long throw, as a matter of fact they measured it up at Elm Park one day, and I was one foot behind Sammy Weaver, who played for Newcastle. He had the longest throw in football – it was 33 yards – and I threw 32 yards 2 ft. I was one foot behind him. It's a knack. I've often tried to tell young lads how to do it, but you can't get them to understand that it starts in your knees, and you transfer it from your knees to your stomach and from your stomach to your shoulders. It's a sort of whiplash action. That's what used to propel the ball. I used to practise it with a medicine ball, and the medicine ball we had in those days was a football case stuffed with steel wool.'

With his obvious talent, it is perhaps surprising that Danny never became a professional. He says simply: 'I had one or two chances but the war killed me. It took me from 20 to 27 which are your best years.'

His last game was against RAF Shinfield in the Wednesday Cup Final at Kensington Road in 1957 and once he made the decision to stop playing he kept to it with the determination he showed throughout his playing life.

'Both my teams had gone, I was 37 going on 38 and I thought to myself, Well, that's as good a time as any, and I've never touched a ball since. I've never even kicked the ball in fun. I just shut the door behind me and it never bothered me.'

Dave Chard and Dave Burbedge

Two well-remembered players from more recent times are West Reading stalwarts Dave Burbedge and Dave Chard.

Dave Burbedge has stayed loyal to West Reading since he was a youngster who signed on from Battle Youth.

Dave is too modest to talk about his playing days but fellow West Reading players Jack Jarvis and Tony Bampton remember the skills of the man they call 'the best amateur footballer the town has ever seen'.

'What can we say about him. There's no doubt about it, as a player he took the breath away of everybody in local football. He was absolutely brilliant. There was nothing that David was weak on, he was a great defender, a great attacker. People went after Dave. Someone asked Jimmy Wheeler, who was manager of Reading at the time, "Why on earth don't you sign Dave Burbedge?" He said, "I've begged him, he doesn't want to know." He just wanted to stay with Tom Raven and West Reading.

'We always think – and Dave will confirm this – that he was worried he wouldn't get back for the dogs on Saturday night if he signed for a professional side! Tottenham was interested in David, Portsmouth was interested in David. But he went on with this side all through the 60s and 70s winning everything.

'Eventually when he got married and needed money for the mortgage, he signed for Wokingham and for two or three seasons he was voted player of the year. He was 27 when he joined them, played for them for three or four years, and then he came back to West Reading. He's been there ever since as a player and over the last two seasons he's taken over as manager.

'Officially he's stopped playing but give him half a chance to be second sub and he'll have his boots on, but I think he's finally accepted it.

'David played until he was 50 and all the young players around today who see him playing in his 40s and 50s have got no idea of how good he was; he was absolutely fantastic. They might think he's an old duffer but he was a fantastic player.'

With the name of Dave Burbedge is linked the name of Dave Chard, another player who came to West Reading from Battle Youth at the age of 18, and later became captain. 'Chardy' and Dave Burbedge were great mates and won at least 100 cups each for Saturday and Sunday football. Jack Jarvis remembers Chardy's early days:

'He was a lovely little quiet chap. I can remember it well, when David came into that first team. We were playing at the track and I had a word with him, this lovely little 18-year-old, and said, "Don't worry about things, Dave." From then on Dave never missed a game for the next 20 seasons. He captained West Reading, he captained Theale Football Club, and he captained the county, the Berks and Bucks. Everyone says Dave Chard was the finest captain you will ever see. He

Dave Chard (top) and Dave Burbedge depicted by Areff

never ever criticised a player, he just gave everybody encouragement. Win, lose or draw, Dave never changed, he was a fantastic captain.

'Having a good captain is the most important thing and a lot of West Reading's success was due to him. There were all the clever ones and all the fast ones, like me, but Dave Chard's captaincy was an example on the field, of effort, of encouragement. He was a leader of men there is no doubt, and everybody in local football knew Dave Chard. If Dave walks around Reading today he will be stopped 30 or 40 times by people saying, "Hi Dave, hi Dave".'

Peter Bartlett adds:

'Dave Chard was tremendous to have in the side because he never stopped trying. I can remember one game when we were playing Tilehurst, and I think it was 1-8 or something and in the last minute Chardy went up and scored from the corner. That was typical Chardy.'

Each year, in October, a reunion of former Reading FC and prominent local amateur players is held at the Curzon Club in Oxford Road, Reading. The first was in 1991 and as well as enabling former players to renew old friendships and reminisce about matches it has also enabled organiser Keith Orwin to raise £1,000 for the Lupus UK research fund. At the most recent reunion in October 1995 there was a squad of 1950s and 60s Reading players that would have delighted any manager.
Pictured above are: (back row) Roger Gabbini, David Jones, John Wicks, George Cryle; (middle row) David Grant, Douggie Webb, Ronnie Blackman, Ray Reeves, Maurice Evans, Bobby Williams, Alan Wicks, Grorge Harris; (front row): Tommy Ritchie, Gordon Neate, Johnny Walker.

5 The Biscuitmen

The Birth of the Blues and Whites

by David Downs

Reading FC was formed in 1871, when the inaugural meeting of the club was held at the Bridge Street Rooms under the chairmanship of Mr James Sydenham, who later became the first Honorary Secretary of the club. The early matches were played at Reading Recreation Ground, and later fixtures were fulfilled at Reading Cricket Ground, Coley Park and Caversham Cricket Ground before the move, on September 5 1896, to Elm Park, which has been the club's home ever since.

In those days the club played only friendly and cup matches, despite having amalgamated with other local clubs, the Hornets and Earley. However, Reading were the first winners of the Berks and Bucks Senior Cup, defeating Marlow 1-0 in the final of the 1877-78 competition. They also appeared in the FA Challenge Cup, and the club's record defeat occurred as long ago as 1894, when they were beaten 18-0 by Preston North End in the first round of that competition.

That same year, 1894, Reading became founder members of the Southern League, formed to answer the demand for a regular fixture list, and in order to improve its playing standards, the club adopted professionalism in 1895. Reading FC was registered as a limited company on August 11 that year, with Mr J B Messer as its chairman. The club's stay in the Southern League was undistinguished, though it won the Second Division Championship in 1911.

Reading Football Club, 1925-26, winners of Division Three, English League

Appearing in the club's colours were Johnny Holt and Herbert Smith, both of whom won England International caps whilst with Reading.

At the start of the 1920-21 season, the Southern League clubs were elected en bloc to form Division Three of the Football League, and

73

in 1925-26, Reading won the Championship of Division Three (South). Promotion was assured with a thrilling 7-1 victory over Brentford, and international honours were gained by Dai Evans for Wales, and by Billy McConnell and Hugh Davey for Northern Ireland.

Richard Johnson, a lad of 17 working at a wholesale grocers in Friar Street, and a keen fan of Reading, vividly remembers the 1925-6 season, the year they gained promotion:

'At that time Reading had a trainer named Jerry Jackson. He was about 5ft 8in, no more, and he was nearly 5ft 8in around. There was also a ref, who came from Bristol, whose name was E E Small. There was no doubt at all, he used to favour Reading. It was most marked. Reading always used to get the benefit of the doubt. As a result E E Small was very popular. He used to be cheered on to the field, and off the field. There's no wonder they won promotion!

'One particular match I remember was against Plymouth Argyle. They and Reading were both heading for promotion to the Second Division, and Reading was playing them away. My sister and I could only accompany them to an away match if we could afford it. My wages in those days were eight shillings a week and I gave my Mum six shillings, so I didn't have much left for football. I think it cost about 12 or 14 bob return on the train to Plymouth; we two kids had a job to scrape it up but we did and we thoroughly enjoyed ourselves.

'Yes. I shall always remember it. Reading won 3-1. It was the first weekend Reading played a new player called Frank Richardson. He came from Swindon Town and took the place of Davey, Reading's international centre-forward in those days. I've still got a picture of that team. I can remember them all now, absolute heroes.

'I suppose Hugh Davey was possibly the best technical player. He was good, very quick, always in the right place at the right time, and he got a tremendous amount of goals. I think my personal favourite was the captain, Bert Eggo. He was getting on in years, well into his thirties when he played for Reading. He was full back, and he was really good, right throughout the year. Eventually, when he retired he took a pub in King's Road, Reading.

'We had a very lively player in the team at that time, Billy McConnell, who was capped for Ireland, but was a dabster at fouls on the quiet. Of course the refs got to know him, and he was sent off several times. When they were fouls in those days, they were fouls.'

The club's best run in the FA Cup came the following season, when they were beaten 3-0 by Cardiff City, the eventual winners, in the semi-final at Wolverhampton. In Round Five,

> *'I miss the old technique of the 1920s and 1930s, when there was more kick and run. I often compare it with what I see today, and of course it's faster now, much faster than it used to be in those days. But it's not all that much more skilled. No, despite all the training they have, and the schools they attend as youngsters, it's certainly not more entertaining. We seemed to get far more thrills in the game than we do now.'*
> *Richard Johnson*

the current attendance record for Elm Park was set, as 33,042 spectators watched Reading's 1-0 victory against Brentford.

Reading lost their place in Division Two in May 1931, and returned to Division Three (South) until the outbreak of World War Two.

A hard life!

During the 30s one of Reading's most consistent players was Joe McGough who was with the club for six seasons from 1932 to 1938, when he moved to Chester. He wrote about those six happy years:

'I arrived for trials at Elm Park on the last day of 1931, and met the manager Joe Smith, trainer Bill Clancy, and assistant trainer Bert Penny. I was taken on and shared digs with Ted Harston, who later went on to Mansfield.

'I was 9 stone 2 pounds when I started at Reading, so I was told to get a bottle of Guinness each night, from the Spread Eagle, which was an off-licence shop then. From then on that was my drink. Joe Smith wouldn't let me lap in training, he would tell me to walk, and then sprint 10 or 20 yards. He would ask me to go out in the afternoon. He would be in goal and I would take shooting practice.

'I had digs just across the road from the dressing rooms in Norfolk Road, and very nice they were too. Jimmy Liddle arrived to share the digs with me. He and I later formed the right wing for the club. I saw him take a penalty once where the ball hit the iron support at the back of the goal and bounced back nearly to the halfway line. One season, when we beat Thames 5-1 at home, I remember Alec Ritchie scored with a shot on the volley which hit the crossbar, then the upright, bounced along the line, hit the other upright, and eventually went over the goal line.

'The team, as I remember it, was usually chosen from Lance Richardson, Mellors, Foster, Hodgkiss, Jock Richardson, Darnell, Allen, Barley, Baggett, Ritchie, Eaton, Palethorpe, and McPherson. I remember that Lance Richardson was a very smart dresser, and would often arrive at the ground wearing a stetson, spats and carrying an umbrella. Players left the club and new ones came. I remember meeting a young chap off the train from Bolton, by the name of Sam Bartram, on trial for a month as a wing half. He went back home, Jimmy Seed saw him the next season in goal, and took him to Charlton where he played for 23 seasons.

'I can remember Matt Foster at full-back with Hodgkiss and Richardson. He had to travel each day from the other side of London, and he could play anything on the piano. The games room under the

'Whenever I think of Reading, Mr Joe Smith and Bill Clancy stand forward.'

Joe McGough

'I liked the pitch at Elm Park. It was like a billiard table, looked after by Sutton's Seeds each summer, and during the season by Old Bart the groundsman, and Baden Smith, his assistant.'

Joe McGough

Cartoonist C S 'Snooper' Jones was following Reading in the 30s. This is a new angle on H J McMahon who played for Reading from 1932-6

stand held a full-sized billiards table, piano, shove ha'penny board, skittles, darts, and card tables. There were some good card players too, George Johnson in particular was one.

'As for the training schedule, we used to have Mondays free, Tuesday mornings we trained at the ground, and in the afternoon walked round Prospect Park to keep us out of the town. Wednesdays the club used to take us to Sonning for a day's golf. Thursdays we would train at the ground again, then walk round the park. On Fridays some players did a few sprints, then some had a massage from trainer Bill Clancy, and some just went out for a walk. Friday afternoon was time to collect our pay. What a hard life we had!

'On Saturday afternoon we played like hell for two points, and a £2 win bonus. I was getting £6 a week when I was in a team, plus £2 for a win and £1 for a draw. A footballer could not get more than £8 a week basic pay even in the First Division, so I never grumbled. Whenever we played, Bill Clancy would pass a bottle of whisky as we were going out, and again at half-time.

'I think one of our best games was against the Arsenal, the lads in the team were only allowed five tickets each, and all your friends and other people were asking you to get them one. I gave mine away in the end. It was a very windy day for the match, and we lost 1-0 - Bastin scored.

'I can remember a game against Millwall one Boxing Day morning, when we won 2-1 after playing the last 15 minutes with only eight men. Charley Barley and Charley Townsend had been carried off injured, and Tommy Tait was sent off by the referee, Mr Denton.

'I was married in 1937, and that season I played four games in five days over the Easter period, and we took seven points out of eight. It should have been eight out of eight, but I had a goal disallowed at Queens Park Rangers.

'At the end of the 1938 season I received a letter from the club telling me that I was on the list at £500. At the time I was the longest serving player, so it was quite a shock. I was out of work for six weeks and never got a penny, because contracts ran from May to May. Then Chester inquired about me and I signed the next day.'

'Of course, football died a death in the war years. We were marching up and down the streets.'

Danny Webb

Reading FC won the Southern Section Cup, beating Bristol City 6-2 on aggregate in the two-legged final of 1938, and seemed set for success in the following season, 1939-40. But national events were to overtake them. What started as an unbeaten season was abruptly terminated. As the Berkshire Chronicle reported disapprovingly on September 8, 1939: 'Club badly hit by war decision.'

6 The Royals
The post-war years

by David Downs

When league football resumed after the war, Reading quickly came to prominence once again. The club's record victory, 10-2 against Crystal Palace, was ahieved in 1946, and Reading twice finished as runners-up in the Third (South), in 1948-49 and 1951-52. In the latter season centre-forward Ron Blackman established the club individual league-scoring record with 39 goals, and Jack Lewis set a Football League record with 15 goals from wing-half. Reading amassed a total of 112 league goals, and two other well-known players in the team were Maurice Edleston, a former amateur international, and Stan Wicks, an England 'B' International.

By finishing fifth in the division in 1957-58, Reading became founder-members of the non-regional Division Three, remaining there until the Centenary Season of 1970-71. This proved to be one of the least successful in the club's history, and at the end of it, Reading were relegated to Division Four on goal average. It took the club five seasons to regain Division Three status, third place and promotion being achieved in 1975-76, but the club slipped back to the Fourth at the end of the following season.

1978-79 brought promotion once again, Reading becoming Champions of Division Four under the managership of Maurice Evans, a former player, and setting another Football League record by not conceding a goal for 1,074 minutes. Steve Death was the goalkeeper throughout that period, and at centre-back was Martin Hicks, who still holds the club appearance record with 577 games in first-class competitions.

In the 1982-83 season, Reading almost ceased to exist. Relegation to Division Four for the third time was bad enough, but the club had to fight off a threatened merger with Oxford United and the sale of Elm Park. Eventually Reading survived, and at the end of the season, Roger Smee, a former player, was installed as chairman. He appointed Ian Branfoot as manager, and under his guidance, Reading returned to Division Three by finishing third in Division Four in 1983-4.

After a season of consolidation, Reading won the Championship of Division Three in 1985-6, returning to

Roger Smee was appointed chairman at the end of the 1982-83 season

Ian Branfoot's team, which cost only £150,000 to assemble, won its twelfth consecutive league game against Newport County and broke the record held by Spurs for a quarter of a century. They won for a thirteenth time but failed to break the all-time record of fourteen consecutive victories

Division Two after an absence of 55 years. The club set a record for the Football League by winning outright its first 13 games, and a club record by totalling 94 points. The game in which they beat the record was against Newport and Norrie Hart was one of more than 4,000 supporters who attended.

'The greatest match I can ever remember, and it's going to sound silly, was when Reading went down to play Newport and they were about to break the record. I wasn't going because I'd got a shop but early on the Saturday morning somebody said to me: "Are you going down to Newport?" and I said, "No, I can't very well because of the shop," and Mags, my wife, said, "I'll cover the shop if you want to go."

'So I'd gone down to Elm Park and I'd got one of the last seats on the coach. It was the first time I'd ever gone by coach – I'm a terrible traveller – and I remember going down to a service area on the M4 and I actually bought a scarf. I hadn't owned a scarf and a rattle since I was a kid but there just happened to be a blue and white scarf in this service area. Back on the coach and I could see all these hoards of people going down the M4, going down to Newport on this Saturday lunchtime.

'We got over the Severn bridge and we had to stop at the end of the M4. The police were absolutely brilliant. All the coaches were held up and we were led into Newport. I got a seat, which isn't hard to get at Newport because their gates were generally 3,500, and I was sitting with several other people who were connected with the club.

'We won 2-0. I can remember Stuart Beavon, who scored the first goal, running over, and I thought he was going to kiss me because he'd given them another step on the ladder to promotion. Then the police led us back out, and there were so many people along the roadside indicating to us what the score was! I got back home and probably for only the fourth time in my life, I got drunk. I must have consumed about five or six pints of cider which is far more than my usual limit. I don't remember an awful lot about it except that game was something special.'

The return to Division Two lasted only two seasons, as Reading were relegated in 1987-88. That two-year spell in Division Two contained, however, what many supporters regard as the club's greatest achievement. Reading reached Wembley for the first time in its long history, beating four Division One teams on the way to the Simod Cup Final. Reading won the Simod Cup, defeating another Division One club, Luton Town, at Wembley, on March 27, 1988, by four goals to one, in front of a crowd of 61,470, at that time the highest attendance at a game in which Reading had played. Norrie Hart remembers it well:

84

The Simod Cup victory – manager Ian Branfoot congratulates the players after the match

'The Simod Cup was a happy memory of football. We took 42,000 to Wembley, and Reading and Luton supporters, before and after the game, all danced together to the steel bands. It was an occasion. On the way through to the final we had great times – we had Coventry, QPR, Oxford United and Nottingham Forest. I saw every one of them. Myself, the wife and my daughter, little Beverley, aged 12, bought all the gear – hats and scarves. We got seats and there was so many people around us, great friends, former players, and there was our kid waving a flag. So we're one goal down and I thought, I'll just sit back and enjoy this, and we went 1-1, 2-1, 3-1, 4-1. And I remember my daughter saying, "Mum, Daddy's crying." I was crying my eyes out. Unbelievable.'

Reading spent several seasons back in Division Two (the former Division Three) until the arrival of John Madejski as chairman and Mark McGhee as manager revitalised the club. Under their leadership, the club became committed to a policy of attractive, attacking football. Steady progress, including the development of a flourishing youth scheme as well as the introduction of several international players to the first team, led to Reading winning the Championship of Division Two in 1993-4. Reading thus became the only club to have won the championships of the Second, Third, Third (South), and Fourth Divisions.

The 1994-95 season in Division One proved to be as traumatic as any in the long history of the club. Reading spent the majority of the campaign in the play-off positions, even the departure of Mark McGhee in December doing little to halt the team's progress. Joint player-managers Mick Gooding and Jimmy Quinn led the side to an eventual second place, the best ever achieved by Reading. Quinn became Reading's most capped International player with 15 appearances for Northern Ireland, and Adrian Williams became a regular in the Welsh team.

In the end of season play-offs, Reading beat Tranmere Rovers 3-1 on aggregate, setting a receipts record of £90,668 for Elm Park in the home leg. The final at Wembley saw Reading take a two-goal lead against Bolton Wanderers before losing 4-3 after extra time. The attendance for the club's second appearance at the national stadium was 64,107, yet another record.

Although there was disappointment at the failure to clear the last hurdle, there is little doubt that Reading Football Club is on the verge of great things. A move to a purpose-built site near the M4 is scheduled for 1997. Promotion to the Premier League and the possibility of European competition are within reach in the foreseeable future. And despite a poor start to the 1995-6 season Reading succeeded in making club history on November 28, 1995, by reaching the quarter final of the Coca-Cola Cup for the first time by beating Premiership club Southampton 2-1 at Elm Park, but were then knocked out by Leeds 2-1.

THE GREATEST SEASON, 1994-95
by Simon Blackburn,

Word on the street during the summer break was that Reading was a definite candidate for relegation – nine months later the club were only four minutes away from joining the élite in the Premier. A cruel end to a season packed with events on and off the field.

The greatest season in the club's history began in a packed Molineux (27,012). The players came out to the ska sounds of the Liquidator, bellowing out from the tannoy in an increasingly hostile atmosphere. Within 10 minutes the Wolves had roared in the first goal. Ninety-five per cent of the ground anticipated this was the beginning of a rout – but how wrong they were! Eighty minutes later we had missed numerous gilt opportunities, and completely outplayed them, yet somehow we lost. On the way out I heard a Wolves' fan say, 'How the hell did we get away with that one?' As for the Royals, it had been a taste of what lay ahead, but with somewhat different conclusions.

Five games later we had won three, and drawn two, conceding only one goal in the process. Our trio of summer acquisitions for a massive total of £90,000 had really settled in well – the imagination and creativity of Simon Osborn, the ice-cool temperament of Dariusz Wdowczyk, and the general sound defending of Andy Bernal had proved McGhee and Lee's credibility with the 'scouting eye'.

Wednesday, 14 September – Swindon (A). Our rivalry with this lot from down the M4 goes back decades – basically we hate each other. They gave us only 1,500 tickets, and these were for revitalised toilet seats behind the goal. As local derbies go, this was a pretty dull affair. However, when Norway clashed with Poland, the latter saw red. Fjortoft is a dirty bastard, and but for the fact that he actually does possess talent, he would have been forced back to his Scandi-homeland ages ago, with a good few hundred boots acting as directives!

Keith Scott came on for Swindon, scored a fluke goal, and then took great satisfaction in nearly setting-up a mini riot by V-signing the Reading contingent.

Come the beginning of October we had got ourselves into third place. As usual we'd got absolutely no coverage from the

Reading Football Club players after the final training session at Egham the day before Wembley on May 28, 1995. Picture by Tim Redgrove

national media. Rave reviews were limited to the local press and the witnessing fans. Playing Notts County in a somewhat drab game, some bloke decided the only·way to set this game alight was to set fire to the stand. This accident held the game up and the fans took refuge on the pitch, while the cause of alarm was located. It was nothing serious, but it had great implications on the season. Super-striker Archie Lovell didn't have time to warm up properly after the stoppage and pulled up with a strain – one of those that take a decade to heal.

A couple of good wins followed, then came the crunch. If we beat Sunderland at home, we'd go top. It poured with rain and we lost 2-0. Jimmy Quinn needed an operation after this game, which should've given McGhee ammunition to seek money off the chairman for a replacement. The outcome – 'No Way'.

McGhee was forced to try various different combinations up front, some of which came off, others totally back-fired on him. He was getting thoroughly pissed off with the whole situation at the club, and before we knew it he was being linked with every vacant managership position. The crunch came playing away at Pompey. The previous day he had been linked with the Leicester job. Over 3,000 made it down to Fratton Park to voice their opinions. By Tuesday morning we thought it had worked.

The local paper proclaimed McGhee's loyalty to the club – 'McGhee to stay'. In reality he had gone, taking with him the assistant manager and the coach. The town was gutted

The local paper proclaimed McGhee's loyalty to the club – 'McGhee to stay'. In reality he had gone, taking with him the assistant manager and the coach. The town was gutted. Somewhere along the line a break-down in communications had led to different readings of the situation. The chairman even contemplated 'knocking it on the head'; he felt betrayed and let down. As usual we fans were the real losing party. It was like a bereavement from which we might never recover.

Our chairman is really into all that 'town spirit stuff' and within days, four of our playing staff (two injured actually) had taken up temporary management roles. The first game was Wolves at home. Not exactly your ideal opponents at the end of a traumatic week. However, it was a chance to prove in football that no-one is irreplaceable.

The chairman walked round the perimeter of the pitch before kick-off, conjuring up support from the packed terraces and stand. Within minutes Elm Park had witnessed Wolves going one-up. Then a mistimed tackle by our Scott Taylor had finished Froggatt for the season, and all of a sudden the game was alive.

way to Elm Park. As I grew I was allowed to say farewell to the New Stand and stand behind the goals. The Supporters' Club (subscription one shilling a year) performed a miracle and produced a small covered section opposite the half-way line Life for someone under 4ft 6ins might have been difficult, but the crowds were always prepared to push us down towards the rails, where we could see our heroes.

I well remember seeing Arsenal – then in their glory days – play at home when we were thrust out of the FA Cup by a glorious volley from Bastin. We had a wonderful half-back line; Johnson, Hayhurst, Wright, with Charley Barley as a mid-field supplement. They flattened Ted Drake and his co-stars that afternoon. Reading were renowned as a fierce, hard-hitting side who were divorced from the niceties of top class football.

As a committed fan, it was my pleasure to watch the lads (as they were always called, regardless of age) as they arrived on match days. Earning £7 or £8 a week, they were hardly in the Public Utility Director class, but in poverty-stricken days they were regarded as being pleasantly well off. They wore, to a man, plus-fours - some flashy, some modest - and they were always fit and filled with stamina. My favourite player ever was Tommy Tait, a centre forward we signed from Bournemouth - a £1,000 fee, would you believe it? - but he was worth every penny. I kept until recently a programme signed by the great man when I cornered him once outside the players' and officials' entrance.

I remember the surge of enthusiasm that followed the buying of Billy Butler, still at that time England's No 7. He eventually took over as manager, but the same success did not follow him in that capacity. He was a wonderful winger, even by third division standards.

Like most supporters I carried on a racy correspondence with the chairman, who was at that time a successful butcher called Lee. After I had written many reproachful letters to him, I finally had a reply. 'I hope it will all be better,' he wrote, 'after a change in managementship.'

'In my younger days I got myself into all kinds of trouble at away matches. We were particularly hated as visitors, especially at Queens Park Rangers, where on one occasion I only just escaped the fighting bodies before the police came charging in.'

David Barr

MY NUMBER ONE LOVE

Norrie Hart is Councillor for the Berks and Bucks FA, and Cup Competitions Chairman for Reading and District Sunday football league, but first and foremost he is a football fan. 'It is my number one interest and I would go anywhere to watch a game.' His greatest love is Reading FC.

'My first recollection was in 1934 at four years old, and my dad took me to Elm Park. I was in a carrier on the back of a bike, and I can remember it distinctly, although it's 60 years ago. The bike went into a place in Kent Road, I was taken out and stuck on his shoulders and we went into Elm Park. I believe the cost in those days was one and six-pence, and I spent most of the game on his shoulders.

'The first game that I can recall was against Norwich, who were play-ing in a very bright yellow – they called the Canaries – and Reading won 1-0. I can remember distinctly the excitement – particu-larly those yellow shirts – and I can see that team coming out of the tunnel. I was actually stood down by the railings when they came out, and my dad lifted me up. My dad kept telling me about the marvellous days when we were in the second division for the first time, and beat Spurs and Sheffield Wednesday in the FA Cup (1928-29).

'One of the biggest problems from then onwards was my dad couldn't always go so I was reliant on uncles and elder cousins to take me down there, but I became a real Biscuitmen fan. When I was a kid they used to put wooden benches all round the touchline for people to sit on and stewards with megaphones shouted out, "Everybody move down". Look at the stewards now. A lot are just in there for a yellow coat and a free match; they are not what they used to be.

'Over that period of time I went whenever someone would take me, until, in my early teens, when I was able to go down on my own and pay my one and six. I have great recollections of walking from Whitley, where I lived, into Reading, as I couldn't afford the fare as well as the fish and chips at Picton's café in St Mary Butt's. I think that was one and six as well – fish and chips, bread and butter and a cup of tea – then the sixpenny bus up to Elm Park. They used to drop us off in the Tilehurst Road and then they'd stay in a line there. It was a special football bus service but then gates were anything from 15,000 to 18,000 a game, sometimes more. They were big gates, and I look back on the last few years, until we became moderately successful, when they struggled to get 5,000 or 6,000.

'In 1952, I came out of the services and back to my number one love – and it still is – Reading Football Club. I totally ignored playing, I wasn't all that good. I supported Reading everywhere I possibly could, went on to every league ground where there was football to be played. I can remember going down to Elm Park for a cup match against Swindon – I lost my job over that. I was working for Brown Brothers, and I went down mid-week to help to sell tickets and somebody split on me. I went to see the governor and it was leave or get the sack, so I left and joined Thames Valley buses.

'Support for Reading has now got back to something like it was, but in

8 Fans and Fanzines

Loyal Royals

THE FANZINES

It has been said that the saviour of football in the last few years has not been the mega-rich chairmen, nor the intense media coverage but the fanzine. It is a magazine written by the fan for the fan and provides an alternative look at the club in the way a fan sees it. In a nutshell - 'When you look out of one window you see one view, but when you go to the other side, things look completely different.'

Reading has had three long-term fanzines over the last ten years, and the following pieces introduce themselves.

ELM PARK DISEASE (August 1988-May 1989)
by Peter Adams

At one time, 'Elm Park Disease' was taken to the hearts of Reading fans along with Martin Hicks' ozone-destroying long balls and Ian Branfoot's Geordie dialect. Both of the latter were mercilessly lampooned in this trail-blazing tome, the lovable Geordie chap appearing as a character called Brian Infoot.

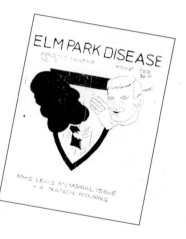

Brian has still been turning on the style at various places, including Southampton, Crystal Palace and Fulham, whose fanzine, 'One F in Fulham', won a competition for the best fanzine title, pushing ours into third place. Gillingham's 'Brian Moore's Head is like the London Planetarium', came second, as a matter of interest. However, third place remained our greatest triumph, thus giving Gerry McGreevy, John Duggan, Niall O'Brien and Peter Adams, the purveyors of this frequently plagiarised work, a full 30 seconds of fame.

'The Disease', as it was affectionately known, was born in the old supporters' club, under the main stand, one boozy quiz night. The birth was painless, but its childhood traumatic, with the editorial team being hunted down by the press and hauled up before club officials. However, we were wily youths and persuaded the club that when it came to Reading Football Club we were as keen as mustard - which was true enough.

The main thrust of our fanzine, though, was to campaign against Colin Moynihan's football membership scheme (Colin who?). Football fans at that time needed to vent their anger in

Players and those who run the game – 'our game' to use one of their clichés – should never be allowed to forget where most of the finance comes from.

a way that matchday magazines could never hope to.

Apart from the time it took to produce 'The Disease', it was probably because the specific aims of the fanzine had been met, that after just over one season the disease was cured - not killed off! The fans' voices should always be there to flare up again. So many fanzines today miss the point – they are today's football hooligans with a DTP facility slagging off other clubs. It only shows how disunited we are.

So, will this precocious fanzine ever appear again? Probably not. Like the Beatles, we and 'The Disease' are yesterday's flavours, yesterday's answers. Someone else must grasp the nettle in the future. If they fail to do this, the descendants of yesterday's revolutionaries will have joined the establishment – and lost.

TAKING THE BISCUIT (Dec 1988-Nov 1992)
by Gary Purser

I was there from the beginning – well thereabouts anyway. TTB, issue 1, hit the streets on Boxing Day 1988, the day our mighty Royals took little Aldershot to pieces 3-1, with the help of a brace by the legendary Mick Tait. My involvement that day was minimal. I helped to sell the fanzine next to the corner shop at the Wantage Road/Waverley Road junction.

Royals in "edible food" fiasco.

As the issues started to flow I became more involved. From issue 2, I was one of the 'loony quartet' that regularly worked right through Saturday nights, usually until about 10am on a Sunday, to key in all the articles and information into our computer at TTB Towers, our secret base in Watford.

Working through the night wasn't so bad. We quite often found we came up with our most inspirational ideas then. Well, we thought it was funny at 4.30 on a Sunday morning. We also had the odd disagreement that seemed to carry the magnitude of World War Three over things like biscuits. We were tired!

My first attempts at actually writing for TTB came about when the editor (Tony Ella) kindly agreed to sponsor (supply T-shirts) for my five-a-side team, '17 Nentori Padwits AFC', who played in the Rivermead five-a-side league. My job was to write match reports (loosely termed) for the magazine. These reports usually (always) ended up grossly exaggerated with little or no bearing on the games, or in fact reality in general. The scores however were always true.

The demise of TTB came about largely because of the work

106

commitments of those who were left compiling and producing the magazine. As there were only the three of us, it was becoming more and more difficult to stay fresh and funny. We wanted to go out at the top – so we did.

HEAVEN ELEVEN (October 1994-)
by Simon Blackburn

I was quietly working my way through a typical Sunday roast at some pub on the way to Oxford when I turned to my mother out of the blue and told her I was starting up a Reading fanzine. To my shocked surprise she (a) bought the idea and (b) bought my lunch. My mum's good like that. She used to be a Sheffield Wednesday supporter when she was young, but now, although she still shows as much affection towards the game as she did as a devoted Yorkshire lass, her heart has a definite blue and white hoop running through it.

The name, 'Heaven Eleven', caused many a curious raised eyebrow when it was revealed as the title for Reading's newest fanzine. The reasons behind the name were quite simple – there weren't any!

The one advantage in this production was that Reading had just gained promotion to the Endsleigh First Division, and interest was high in the community. Criticism was hard to make as the team were performing on the field, as were the fans off it, and a more lighthearted read, with a strong leaning towards the humorous side, would provide its supposed content. Whether this has been the reason behind its popularity only the reader can answer. The fanzine has always remained at its launch price of 50p, and when you compare that with other more official merchandise, the price is a bargain in itself.

There's no denying the time needed to put together each issue sometimes doesn't justify logic – but when you avoid the half-time 'Burger King Shootout', and take a swift look around you and see fans chuckling to themselves as they read your production, it all seems worth it!

The first day it came out we were at home to Sunderland, I remember distinctly it poured with rain, we got beat 2-0 but all fanzines went like hot cakes, I would like to think that each issue gets better and if it doesn't – tough!

THE FANS

When do fans become fanatics and why? For local football pundit, 'Barney Rubble', it started when three temporary council workers came to do some house painting in Charvil; for others it was the 1966 World Cup victory or that first visit to Elm Park with dad or uncle.

UNDER THE INFLUENCE
by Barney Rubble

I suppose it's fair to call me a football fanatic. Over the years I've played school football, youth football, progressed into the now defunct Reading Minor League and finally played in the Reading and District League (Saturdays) and the Reading Sunday League. All that time I have been a regular at Elm Park and also watched Wokingham Town and, in their pre-league days, Wycombe Wanderers. Throw in a few Reading reserve games and England internationals, plus all the televised matches and you would be correct in surmising that football has had a major impact upon my life. But how did my fascination with the world's greatest game come about ?

'Talk to most people of my age who like football and they would probably cite England winning the 1966 World Cup as the event which most influenced their childhood love of the game. '

Barney Rubble

Talk to most people of my age who like football and they would probably cite England winning the 1966 World Cup as the event which most influenced their childhood love of the game. It was the start of a golden era for the game in this country with increased attendances, more media coverage and the birth of footballing 'superstars'. However, my own moment of destiny came two or three years before.

At the time I was a youngster living in the sleepy village of Charvil, some six miles outside Reading. Although I'd kicked a ball around with friends I certainly wasn't hooked on football the way I was to be after the 'event', and I had never been to a live game.

At that time professional players were not earning anything like the money that was to be on offer just ten tears later, let alone the grossly inflated wages of today's stars. Players got a winter wage and a summer wage, the summer wage considerably less than the winter reflecting the lack of income for clubs during the close season. Most players were forced to take temporary summer jobs to supplement their meagre income - small wonder that the players rebelled against the maximum wage and other restraints in the following years.

But it was due to the fact that several Reading players had taken summer jobs that I was present at the occasion which was to shape most of my future leisure time. For three Reading players were employed by Wokingham Council to paint the outside of our council houses in Charvil. And who came to paint my house? Denis Allen, that's who!

Denis 'Daisy' Allen playing in a testimonial game

People younger than myself may not appreciate the excitement I felt at this; suffice to say that Denis was already a star at Elm Park and he went on to grace the team until the turn of the decade. Needless to say my schoolmates were as jealous as hell when I rushed home after lessons to talk football to my own professional footballer/painter, and come the school holidays my popularity knew no bounds, with friends coming from miles around to call on me - and Denis. When he finished painting my house we followed him next door while he worked there, and so on down the road.

Quite what Denis made of it all I've no idea but to his credit he never seemed to get fed up with us kids getting under his feet all day, asking him no doubt stupid questions. In fact he enthused us all with his evident love of the game to the point where my mates and I became stalwart regulars at Elm Park from the following season onwards, cheering in the Biscuitmen in their all-sky blue kit and willing Denis Allen to score every time he ventured forward. (Although not a regular goal scorer, he weighed in with a respectable total most seasons as I recall, mainly from his fiercely struck free kicks and long shots.)

Star about the house

'Daisy' Allen, as he was inexplicably nicknamed, remained a hero to me right up to his retirement. And while some of his extended family have become more famous than him and played for more fashionable clubs than little Reading, I always thought of him as the original and the best Allen.

When you look back on any given period, certain players spring to mind and to me at least Denis Allen is always the first name I recall when thinking of Reading in the 1960s. In fact so great was Denis's influence on an impressionable child that I can no longer recall with certainty the names of the other two Reading players who were painting Charvil that summer. In retrospect, I might have got some more out of meeting Denis Allen had I been a few years older and more able to appreciate having a 'star' about my house. But then his influence on me may not have been so great and I might have missed out on the many years of enjoyment I've had from playing and watching football. So it was with genuine sadness that I read of his death.

Thanks for the memories, Denis, childhood hero, professional footballer and painter.

'When you look back on any given period, certain players spring to mind and to me at least Denis Allen is always the first name I recall when thinking of Reading in the 1960s.'

Barney Rubble

THE TEAM

The team, the team,
that's everybody.
Supporters are the life
blood of the team
and the game, ye see!
It's that easy.

We laugh, we share, we
care, we love
skills and team spirit,
camaraderie.
It's a part of that
beautiful game called
football, ye see!

Individual skill, team
work, organisation,
creativity to bring every-
one in harmony.
It ain't easy.

But when you get the
spirit of unity, everyone
appreciating each other,
that goal, that save, the
joy, the sorrow, the pain,
Only your team, your
team gives you those
memories.

Whether it may be
Liverpool, Man United.,
Newcastle, Arsenal,
Tottenham, York,
Rangers, Celtic,
AC Milan, Reading,
AFC Whitchurch.
Only your team gives
you those memories, ye
see!

From The Team
by M C Naptalie

THE LIFE OF A ROYAL
by Michael Welch

Supporting a small, lower division football club such as Reading can make you the butt of many a joke. I don't mind taking a bit of stick. In fact, I quite enjoy the banter, and am more than prepared to offer my own. What gets up my nose, however, are the people who choose to 'support' clubs such as Liverpool or Man United, and take every opportunity to slag off their local team, criticising them even though they never watch them play. Then again, many of these big club parasites haven't even seen their 'own' team play. How many of those supporters have actually been to Anfield or Goodison Park? And isn't it strange to see so many Blackburn Rovers shirts being worn around town? Can you remember seeing one Blackburn shirt in Broad Street two or three years ago? I can't.

The funny thing is these people only seem to mention football to you at work on a Monday morning if Reading have lost. Until, that is, the club looks like achieving a modicum of success. Then it would appear that these people undergo some kind of magical transformation. Suddenly, they can be found on the terraces of Elm Park claiming to be 'Loyal Royals'. The Monday morning conversation is now about how 'we' are going to win the championship. Don't get me wrong, I'm glad that they are now on our side. I only wish they would be there every game, but please, spare me the hypocrisy.

So why on earth do I support Reading through thick and thin? Well, first and foremost, Reading is *my* town. I have lived here for all my life and feel a certain loyalty to the place, even if it did have a reputation for being a bit of a dump.

I was brought up on a council estate in Southcote where there were a lot of other kids of my own age. We would spend most of our time kicking a ball around in the street or at the local playing field, but most of the others would be wearing their Chelsea or Arsenal shirts. Not me. I found it hard to understand why they weren't proud to wear the blue 'n white hoops. I guess they felt that playing the likes of Hartlepool and Doncaster every week was nothing to be proud of. But for me it was inconceivable that I should support any team but Reading.

At the time, Reading Football Club did very little to encourage kids along to Elm Park. There was no involvement with the local schools that there is today. It is therefore reassuring to see many more youngsters now wearing their Reading shirts with pride. Of course, the recent success of the club on the pitch has had much to do with that. But so too has the attitude of the club itself through its involvement in the community. If we are to retain the interest of these youngsters and build a support for the future, then it is vital that Reading Football Club is seen as an extension of the community itself.

I have been brought up on a diet of RFC ever since my dad first took me to watch 'the Biscuitmen' when I was knee high to a grasshopper. I can't actually remember anything about that first game, except the excitement of simply being there. It wasn't long before I was hooked and would continually ask my dad, 'When are we going again dad?'

My uncle also had a big influence on the development of my interest in football. If Reading were playing away, he would take me to watch Aldersh*t at the recreation ground. I think he found it embarrassing sitting in the stand next to me cheering for Reading. The home supporters were obviously very amused by it all. But these excursions gave me the taste for away games, and I desperately wanted to go to places such as Scunthorpe to see Reading play, rather then Aldersh*t versus Crewe. Eventually my mum had to concede to my constant pestering and I was allowed to go to away games. Now I felt like a true supporter, as if I belonged, and was part of the club itself. I just couldn't get enough of watching my heroes.

The big crunch came on the day of my sister's wedding. Reading were playing at home to Rochdale and I knew where I would rather be. Of course I was expected to attend the big family occasion. Needless to say, I went to Elm Park. My mum couldn't believe that I'd miss my own sister's wedding, but I didn't think my sister cared too much. Although my mum has now forgiven me, I've never been allowed to forget it.

Reading Football Club is in my blood. Your emotions can take over completely when standing on the terrace supporting your team. It's as if you become a completely different person for a few hours. Following the Royals has given me many fond memories, and some sad ones too. But you can't just give up on your team in times of trouble. The tough times only make the good ones even more enjoyable.

WHERE DID SCARVES AND BOBBLE HATS GO ?
A fan's reflection on changing times at Reading FC
There has been a massive change at Reading Football Club in the last years, just as there has been a change at nearly every

'If we are to retain the interest of these young-sters and build a support for the future, then it is vital that Reading Football Club is seen as an extension of the com-munity itself.'
Michael Welch

other club in the country. The change I am referring to is not the crazy culture of high transfer fees, nor the big names we see turning out for the most dull-sounding opposition. It's not even the speculation over who on the team will be next to copy Gazza's blond/black/heaven-knows-what hair rinse. No, the change I am referring to is something much more profound. It is the coming of age of the football shirt.

As you look across the Southbank at a home match, or the away end as we travel the country, what do you see? You see one Reading shirt, then another, and another. And then you realise the whole damn crowd have got them on. Next you realise the majority of opposing fans are all wearing their team colours too. (That is apart from Man United fans, who have got so many shirts now they have forgotten which team colours they are to identify with!)

Some of you will ask, 'But why the death of the scarf and-bobble hat?' Others may think you already know the answer. 'It's because football today is supported by those with the money and so everyone can now afford to buy the £40 shirt,' I hear you cry. However, I believe there is more to it than that, and to understand this properly I need to transport you back to the Elm Park terraces of fifteen years ago.

So here we are back in the good old days where my school mates and I cut our football-supporting teeth. 'Wait a minute,' you say, 'how can we have gone back in time? Elm Park doesn't look any different?' We have to hand it to Reading; it's the only up-and-coming club giving the fans today the same quality of facilities they had to put up with in the time before the birth of our Lord Robin Friday.

Okay, so Reading's facilities may exist in a time warp, but there is something that tells us we are back in another era. That something is the anxiety and fear you can sense from the supporters all around you as you now stand on the Southbank on a cold November evening – and this is felt at a mid-week league match at home to Fulham for heaven's sake !

We see the old men standing with their coat collars turned up against the wind, shuffling from foot to foot like Emperor penguins in an Antarctic blizzard, the kids chewing bazooka gum as they continually tie and re-tie their scarves around their wrists, and the scowling young men nervously awaiting the call to arms as the cry of 'T-T-THE R-R-READING!' goes up to taunt the opposing fans gathering at the back of the Southbank.

Then suddenly half a dozen of Fulham's finest charge from the top scattering fans before them like frightened sheep. The die is cast for a first half of very minor skirmishes, major vocal battles and precious little quality football. At half time the police move in and order is restored. The game winds inexorably on towards the final whistle, and the inevitable nil-nil draw, as Reading's battle-hardened heroes start up the taunts of 'We'll see you all outside' to the opposing fans. These can now be found surrounded at one side of the terrace by a thin line of extra hard-looking police. Old timers and regulars alike mutter that the next time Reading play, they will settle down in front of the telly instead of turning up to this kind of 'entertainment' again. However, you know they said that the last time, and they will still keep coming back like clockwork week after week.

Now picture a bright counter piled high with faithful copies of Reading's latest team strip fifteen years later. So how come everybody is buying the shirt today after those bitter memories?

I believe it's all to do with the fact that people today are actually enjoying going along to watch Reading play. They are therefore identifying more with the club, and this leads to a real feeling of pride in the team. And quite obviously if they feel this sense of association they are then going to want to advertise the fact as much as possible. What better way to do this than by wearing the team shirt? Why have five minutes of 'You'll never walk alone' with a scrap of cloth you've got to untie from around your neck (unless you're a Liverpool fan of course, when you really can't afford the shirt). Instead, wearing your new blue and white shirt, you can sit there for a full 90 minutes exposing the team's colours across your chest.

I also see a lot of fans up and down the country now showing a real sense of pride in their clubs. Fans sit in wonder, looking out over a totally refurbished all-seater stadium from their comfortable seats high up in the stand, and they feel mighty proud. If you don't believe me, just go to Wolves or Huddersfield. Add to this the absence of violence erupting all around them, as well as the fact that the team might also be playing some good football, and suddenly going along to a match starts to become an enjoyable experience.

Now the phrase 'comfortable all-seater stadium' is not one Reading fans can associate too well with in describing their own cathedral for football. However, during the mid-eighties

As a 10th birthday treat Emma Trenchard was mascot for the day on February 4, 1995, when Reading FC played Middlesbrough away, beating them 0-1. It was one of the last matches at Ayresome Park before Middlesbrough moved to its new stadium. Emma (pictured above with Jeff Hopkins) comes from a family of Reading fans. Her grandmother worked in the club office and Reesy and Jon Trenchard actually met at an away match.

*'If the drive and ambi-
tion continue, who
knows what is waiting
for Reading FC?'*

the atmosphere at just about every football ground, including Elm Park, began to improve. Where things were beyond all hope, for example at Millwall, grounds were closed completely and new ones built.

At Reading FC there began to develop a new mood of optimism in both club and supporter alike. This had its roots in the flirtation with what was then the old Second Division in 1986-87, flowering briefly into that amazing visit to Wembley in March 1988 for the Simod Cup final. Forty thousand Reading fans discovered two things that day: firstly that success was achievable, and secondly that it made you feel very proud indeed and you wanted more of it.

Later under Mark McGhee, players developed the art of keeping the ball on the deck and the one touch pass, and used this revelation to score more goals than the opposition and so win matches. (So simple it makes you wonder why they hadn't thought of it sooner.) The players realised that they didn't need the 'Fat Round One' to show them how to play, and so they continued up the league. This style of play took the club to what was probably one penalty kick away from the holy grail of the Premiership in 1994-95, playing the type of football the fans actually wanted to watch. If the drive and ambition continue, who knows what is waiting for Reading FC?

So there you have it. Even without a new all-seater stadium, Reading fans have been flocking to buy the team shirt to show their allegiance to the club - matches like those against Fulham long ago but a distant memory.

And, as for the bobble hat, if you still don't know what brought about its demise, just fish it out from the bottom of your cupboard, and put it on in front of the mirror. There, you can answer that one for yourself, can't you?

9 Crossing the barriers

Women in football

by Alison Haymonds

Women's football has been played on and off in Reading since the early part of the century although it is only in the last eight years that the game has really taken off, with the first girls to have played continuously from age of 11 now competing in senior football. But women have been involved in the local football scene at all levels and the town can boast one women's international, Terri Hinton; the first woman to be a Class One referee in the area, Alison Chapman; and the first female general manager in the league, Annie Bassett.

The first women's games on record were a series of three friendly matches between Reading Ladies and Swindon Ladies in 1921 from which Reading emerged undisputed champions. The first leg took place on Good Friday at Elm Park and was a benefit match for Reading FC's fine player Joe 'Bubbles' Bailey. There had already been a benefit match between Reading and Plymouth Argyle which raised £362 and the huge crowd – 9,000 – who watched Reading Ladies win 6-0 must have boosted the purse satisfactorily.

The two sides met again at Swindon when Reading won again 5-0, and the final match was held on May 16 at Reading Football Club's Whit Monday fete at Prospect Park. Once again Reading triumphed 1-0 and the ladies proved a great draw, though more as an entertaining sideshow than a serious game, according to the contemporary newspaper report :

The ladies' match between Reading and Swindon created tremendous interest and so numerous were those desiring to see the game that it was only with the greatest difficulty that a space was cleared for the match to take place. Even then the crowd were many yards on the wrong side of the touchline. Handicapped by the smallness of the arena, it was impossible for the girls to give of their best but the display was very entertaining and Reading won a good game by a goal to nothing. The goal was a humorous affair, the Reading centre-forward bustling the Swindon goalkeeper into the net, ball and all, from a well-placed corner.
The Berkshire Chronicle, May 28, 1921

Traditionally football in Britain has been seen as a man's game. It was reported in The Times (December 6, 1921) that the FA Council thought it unsuitable for women and they should not be encouraged to play

'I think the advent of ladies' football and lady referees is good because it is turning the sport away from the hooligan element, and more towards families. We are getting a better spirit with the young ladies than we've had in men's football for a while .'
Roland Ford, chairman of Reading Town FC

The Whitsun ladies' match seems to have been something of a tradition. In the offical programme for 1928 of Reading Sports Week, held at Palmer Park from Whit Monday, May 28, to Saturday, June 2, one of the main attractions was a football match between two ladies' teams, Mr T Lawrence's X1 and Mr A Truss' X1.

Huntley & Palmers team, circa 1923

There is an old photo of a ladies' football team, described as a Huntley & Palmers Ladies' team, in the H&P works magazine, First Name News (September 1964). This team, says the caption, was 'so good that it was chosen in about 1923 to play in a benefit match for a Reading footballer of that time' and included a Miss Edie Sadler who provided the photo. However the ladies are wearing what look like Reading FC stripes and the football has 'All for Joe' painted on it, so it is more likely to be the team which played for Bubbles Bailey.

NATIONAL GAME

There is little recorded football in the area until the 60s but this reflects what was happening in the rest of the country. Women's football in Britain has lagged behind other countries, mainly because there has been no tradition of girls playing football at schools. The more egalitarian Scandinavians were the first to have a National team in 1970 and the women's game has been far stronger in Norway (they were the 1994 Women's World Cup winners), Sweden, Denmark, Germany, and Italy, which has the only professional women players. America also has a strong tradition of college football.

The FA Women's Challenge Cup competition started in 1969 but it was not until the 90s that the Football Association, which had long given the women's game the cold shoulder, took it over, no longer able to ignore its tremendous growth over the last few years. There is now a national FA Premier League which covers the whole country, with teams from North and South and the Midlands, and also north and south premier divisions which feed the national Premier League. There are 30 women's teams playing at national level.

Elm Park was the first football league ground to stage a women's international in November 1973 when England beat Holland 1-0. Ten years later a second international was held there as part of the first European national competition for ladies and again England won, beating Northern Ireland 6-0.

READING LADIES

Reading's first permanent women's team was the brainchild of Ann Bell, then wife of Reading FC player Terry Bell, who started Reading Ladies in 1970 with Jan Morgan, wife of another Royals player Stuart Morgan, to raise money for charity. Soon the team became more serious and they played for several seasons, managed by Elm Park DJ Roger Ebben. Ann, now Mrs Grosfort, recalls how it started:

The original Reading Ladies team in 1970. Ann Bell is third from left (front row) and Donna Eustace is extreme right (back)

'It all began when I decided, for some unknown reason, that it would be a good idea to start up a ladies' team. I thought, if the men were playing football, why shouldn't the ladies? I also wanted to get publicity to raise money for charity. Stuart and Jan Morgan were good friends of ours so we roped them in. There were a few other Reading FC wives but they all dropped out after the first couple of games.

'I had never played before and I wasn't sporty. I just fancied playing football after being so involved with the game. The first game was on October 25, 1970, the day before my 21st birthday. I can remember missing an open goal in that first game. I don't think there was even a goalie there – and I missed it. I must have been nervous.'

The match was played against Queen's Park Rangers at Scours Lane, Stuart Morgan was referee, and Terry Bell was manager. Reading lost 5-1 but they raised about £100 in aid of Dr Barnado's Homes.

In that first team was Donna Eustace, who played football for many years but has now switched to women's rugby. She was only 15 when she joined Reading Ladies.

'I saw a piece in the Post about the team so I went along to training and was selected for the very first game. I played from then on. I'd always wanted to play. I've got two brothers and I used to kick around in the garden with them. There weren't any other women playing locally.'

In the early matches Reading Ladies borrowed the Royals' reserve team kit. 'But we had to buy our own boots,' said Ann. Donna recalls:

'It was really strange for a girl to go and buy a pair of football boots then. You got looked at as though you were from another planet. Within a few years it was completely different. I can remember my mum being horrified. It finishes her off now I'm playing rugby.'

Ann only played for half a season. She said, 'I enjoyed it. It was really good fun to start with but it got serious and I was

'Reading's footballing lassies made their debut before a crowd so big that it would have pleased the officials at 10 average amateur matches. Their opponents were connected with another league club whose womenfolk have decided to try and prove they can do one better – Queen's Park Rangers.'

Reading Evening Post, October 26 ,1970

'In those early days it was a bit hit and miss – it was hunting in packs. Wherever the ball was there were 22 women.'

Donna Eustace

'I was captain to begin with, obviously – my ball, my team! I was the only centre forward not to score a goal in my entire career. I gave up after half a season, I was such rubbish, sad really. I used to play in my false eyelashes and bouffant hair!'

Ann Grosfort, founder of Reading Ladies

Donna Eustace (left) watches without enthusiasm as 'starlet' Donna Reading kicks off in a charity match in 1971

useless, so I stepped down gracefully and left it to the likes of Donna.' But she still has links with the game. Her son Nicky has joined Reading FC's YTS.

Reading Ladies started as a entertaining way to raise money for charity but quickly uncovered a growing demand by local women for a chance to play seriously. Donna remembers there was no shortage of players.

'There were an awful lot of people who turned up and wanted to play. They came from all backgrounds and were really enthusiastic. If it had been managed properly by Roger Ebben I think it could have taken off in a big way and been one of the main teams in the country. But we always dragged behind the London clubs.

'When I was 16 I went to Loughborough College with another player from Reading Ladies, Wendy Prior, for England trials, but we were both considered too young.'

The Ladies' second season, 1971-2, was their most successful: they were runners up in the Home Counties League, Division 2, runners-up in the Chronicle Cup, and winners of the Youth Bonanza six-a-side. Donna was top goal scorer with 42 goals.

They played teams like Crystal Palace, who were the top side of the day; Bracknell, which had two teams, Bracknell, Bullitts and Bracknell Ladies who eventually merged; Maidstone, and Amersham. They went on tour in Holland and Germany in 1972 and when they played at Ryde on the Isle of Wight they were watched by the largest crowd ever to have watched a football match on the island at that time.

Donna continued to play for Reading for a couple of years.

'There were a lot of problems and a personality clash between two people who wanted to run it, so it split. Judith Jay and I signed for Bracknell in October 1972 but our first game was against Reading and a block was put on us playing, supposedly because of a registration technicality.'

Reading Ladies didn't last much longer and split. Some players went to Bracknell, others to Amersham. Donna eventually finished her soccer career with Newbury.

NEW READING LADIES

It was not until 1988-89 that Reading Ladies were resurrected. Cathy Holwill, secretary for the past three years, and one of only two of the earliest players who are still with the club, joined in 1989 when Anne-Marie Froud was running the team.

'I saw a notice asking for new players and although I had never played football, in fact I hadn't played any sport since school apart from some badminton, I thought it would be a good idea. The first time I turned up I had to play because they were short but I enjoyed it and I've stayed ever since.'

The club were in Divison Three of the South Regional League – there were only three divisions at that time – and played at Prospect Park. In Cathy's first season Reading Ladies were promoted to Division Two but they are now back in the Third Division.

Most of the action has been off the pitch in the intervening years. The club treasurer departed with several thousand pounds and although the club took her to court and won, many players left as a result.

Another burst of publicity came when one of the players Martine Hewitt had a sex change, became Paul Hewitt and wrote a book about her experiences as a transsexual, A Self-Made Man. As Martine she played football at Little Heath Comprehensive School, and at Bath University before joining Reading Ladies. In her first season she scored 25 goals, and in her second, 1991-2, she scored 50 league and cup goals, was leading goal scorer in the Women's Southern League, and won the Players' Player of the Year award.

Things are more stable now. The club, managed by Tyrone Edwards, plays at Berkshire County Sports ground, altbough they have to train at Palmer Park. They are still affiliated to Reading FC, although it's a very loose connection, and they are loyally sponsored each year by local companies. They have a respectable following 'about as many as watch an average men's match'. Players' ages range from 20 to 35 and unlike some clubs Reading Ladies actively encourages players without previous experience. 'We don't take it too seriously but obviously we don't like to get beaten,' said Cathy.

Cathy is very forthright about reports that the women's game is growing dramatically.

'That's complete tripe. We are constantly trying to get more players and this season although we have more than ever before signing on, it's still only 23. That's not a lot in a town this size. Not having a youth team to draw on is a big failing.'

GIRLS' FOOTBALL

It was the younger girls who led the invasion into the male world of football, girls like Debbie Fry, now herself the mother of eight-year-old Petra, a keen footballer who likes to join in

'The only professional team to involve women as an affiliated part are Arsenal, the others don't want to know. It wasn't until a couple of seasons ago Bert Millichip accepted women's football and decided to help. Rugby's completely different; they take you on board and you are part of their club and they will do anything to help.'

Donna Eustace

The most successful team in the area is Binfield, which ,unusually, has always been run by women; the oldest is Newbury which was founded in 1968 as Newbury Golden Eagles and is still going strong

119

with the boys at Geoffrey Field Junior School. About 20 years ago Debbie and her friends at Gorse Road Junior School struck a blow for equality.

'I used to play football when I was little. Not a lot of people know that! We had a big thing going about why girls weren't allowed to play football. The teachers didn't let us do it because we were petite little girls, and if we got kicked we'd get hurt. But we got the boys involved and we had a big discussion at school and in the end they let us do it.

'So they kitted us all out in these little knee pads and arm pads and spiked boots and we went off on the playing field in our green shorts and yellow T-shirts. It was quite unusual in those days. I was lucky because I was so short I was able to wiggle my way in. When the boys were running around kicking the ball, if I wanted to get through somewhere really quick I used to run through the boys' legs on my hands and knees.

'We played in the school with the boys until they got fed up with it. I think they got a bit boisterous and we were starting to get hurt, with big bruises on our arms and legs, so we ended up going back to art and music, back to the dollies!'

But it was a few more years before the first girls' football team was formed due mainly, it seems, to an 11-year-old girl called Lisa Collins.

READING ROYALS

The story does vary in the telling. Doug Cunningham, founder/manager, remembers:

'There had been nothing before then in Reading for girls, it was just boys. I used to run a boys' team in Twyford and I had never been involved in girls' football, in fact I couldn't imagine girls playing.But there was this little girl, 11 years old, who put constant pressure on me to start a girls' team. This was Lisa Collins, and I used to get fed up with it. So I said, "You go and get 18 girls' names and I'll start a team." I thought that would get rid of her. I think it was two days after she came knocking on my door with a list of 23 girls. So that's how we started in November 1987.'

Lisa, now 18 and at Brunel University, remembers it slightly differently.

'I must have been about eight when I started being interested in football. My dad, Ray, had been manager of a boys' football team, Twyford Comets, for about five years from about 1986 to 1992. I used to train with them and I sometimes played friendlies for them. Once my dad put me on at half-time and the manager said, "Oy, get her off, she's too good." I was about 11 at the time.

'At Polehampton Junior school I used to play in the playground with the boys. We had one six-a-side tournament at Woodford Park in Woodley which we won, but that was just a one off. They never let me play in the boys' team in league matches or anything.

'Doug heard about me – he's our window cleaner – and he said, "Do you fancy starting up a girls' football team?"So I said, "Yes, great." I was pretty keen. He asked me to get some names, so he advertised the team in the paper and I got a few friends to come along from school who were interested and it all started from there.'

Whoever was responsible for idea, Twyford Comets Girls, or Reading Royals as they soon became, was the first junior women's football club for girls at under-16 level in the Thames Valley and south of England and was for many seasons the most successful. It is still one of the top teams, and in their first three years at senior level lost only four league games – all to the same team, Swindon Town.

But in their first season they had to organise friendlies against boys' teams a year younger because there were no girls' teams to play. They got thrashed to start with, but soon they started turning the tables. Doug said:

'The boys were great when they were winning but when the girls started beating them the dads started getting a bit nasty saying, "Those girls are older than the boys," and things like that. I kept advertising in the paper for girls' teams, and a team in Tilehurst, Barton Rovers, phoned me up and asked me what they had to do, and I said, "Just get the girls together and we'll give you a friendly." '

This was the start of a two-way tournament which continued during the 1988-9 season. The teams were so evenly balanced that after seven games the cup was shared. It was during this time that Alan Glenny, who later became secretary of the club, first became caught up by women's football.

'I took my daughter to watch them play Barton Rovers and it all hinged on the last game. I seem to remember one team went into the lead, then the other , all very exciting, and it ended up as a 2-2 draw. Everybody was absolutely enthralled, including myself. They showed they've got the same skills as the boys, potentially. They tend to play football not kick each other and shout at each other and pull each other around as boys do. I've seen boys' games end up in an absolute fracas.

'The boys can play hockey at school but we don't seem to be able to play their sport.'

Lisa Collins

'Sometimes you get a few people watching, sometimes you get just a bunch of lads watching to take the mick. I suppose they are surprised how good we are. People aren't interested in girls playing football, it's just not natural according to them. So they don't bother to come and watch.'

Lisa Collins

Reading Royals team pictured in December 1994

'I always say you get more football for your money at women's football. They have got all the skills and they are not knocking each other over every five minutes as the men do.'

In July 1989 the club was renamed Reading Royals Ladies FC and Doug Cunningham started the Thames Valley Girls' League (which folded in 1994). In the first season the Royals won the divisional and cup competitions under the captaincy of Emily Wilkinson, 18, who has played with the club for nearly 10 years and has been captain since she was 11.

'Doug Cunningham told me to turn up for training and when he saw me play he said, "She is what I have been looking for." Lisa Collins was playing then and we were the same standard. Everyone else played like girls. I think that's when Doug became hooked.

'I loved it. Playing football gave me the best days of my life. When I first went training, it was so exciting because it was something I had always wanted to do. I had been so jealous of the boys going off to their football and I was left on my own. I looked forward to Sundays all week.

'At first we played friendlies and then we started the Thames Valley Girls' League. The game I remember best is the first tournament we ever won. We were playing age groups way above us and we were losing all the time. Then we played Arsenal in the Brent Sunbowl five-a-side tournament and we beat them. After that we started winning.

'We've been playing together as a team for years now. We know each other so well and we know each other's game. We have good individual players and we play well as a team. We take our football seriously. All the players have good personalities and we get on well socially. There is no problem with boyfriends. If they don't like you playing football, they aren't worth bothering about. My boyfriend loves me playing football particularly since he gave it up at a young age. One of the girls' boyfriends did say, "Girls can't play football", but he came to watch and couldn't believe it. After that he came to training every time.

The Royals under-16 side swept all opposition aside for several seasons. They were the only club in the southern region to win the WFA Regional Five-a-Side three years running at under-16 level. Doug recalls one highlight:

'In our first season in the southern region under-16s league we beat Waterlooville 31-0. It was such a small pitch, everybody was compacted but we still managed to play football and run circles round them.'

The club expanded to four teams in 1992-3 and the following year the senior team won promotion in their first season

122

from the Southern Region Division Four and took the Division 3/4 plate with a 5-1 victory over Third Division Champions Leighton Linslade. In 1994-5 they lost only two games, finished runners-up to their old adversaries Swindon Town and were promoted to Division Two. This season, 1995-6, is their third at senior level yet the average age of the girls is still only 18.

Doug Cunningham is still president of the Royals Club which now fields six teams, a senior team, senior reserves, under-15s, under-13s, and under-12s A and B teams. They have a new home for they have linked up with Reading Town FC and now play at Scours Lane.

One of their young stars is 10-year-old Rachel Dowling, in her last year at the Westwood Farm County Junior School. Early in the 1995-6 season Rachel scored 10 goals for the Royals Ladies under-12s when they crushed Abbey Rangers under-12s 19-0. Rachel is also a regular member of her school team, the only girl in a squad of 14.

Rachel Dowling – 10 goals

The summer of 1995 was a stormy one for the club and resulted in one team breaking away. Temporarily called Thames Valley Ladies, the new club, managed by Alan Glenny, former secretary of the Royals, plays in the Southern Region, Division Four, and has now changed its name to Wokingham Town Ladies.

Clive Baskerville, of the Reading Evening Post, says that women's football has "blossomed out of all recognition in recent years'.

'Reading Royals, Reading Ladies, Caversham, Barton Rovers and Thames Valley all play on a regular basis. Yet there are still many who don't treat them too seriously, Okay, some may be lacking in the finer arts of the game but these young ladies certainly boast the basic skills and there is no doubting their enthusiasm. '

And Lisa Collins remembers her playing days fondly.

'I've never regretted a minute of it. Running round for an hour and a half is better than anything for keeping you fit. Speed and strengthwise we're not up to the men's standard but we're just as skilled as them.'

Wokingham Town FC has a thriving youth programme and holds soccer fun days, with training sessions and short matches, at the Finchampstead Road ground every Sunday morning for boys and girls aged five and above

THE REFEREE

Alison Chapman, 21, was the first female Class 1 referee in this area. She is in her sixth season, is a ref in the Chiltonian and Allied Counties Youth League and Reading Saturday leagues, and runs the line in the Isthmian League.

'When I started refereeing seven years ago I was about 14, and at that time there weren't many lady players. I've been watching Reading since I was eleven. I used to go with my Grandad and I really loved it. I couldn't play it. I used to knock a ball around with my mates and my brother but I was absolutely hopeless. I wanted to do something, but what could I do? So I thought, I'll referee. I told a few people, and they said, "You'll never do that", so I said, "Okay, just watch this then." That was that.

'I phoned up Reading Football Club and said, "I want to be a referee; do you know anywhere I can go on a referees' course?" They gave me a name to phone, so I did a 10-week course, learning the rules of football – I was the only woman. At the end of it there was a written exam and an oral exam. I passed them, and then I could go out and referee.

'To be controversial about the women's game: women's football is okay when you get up to the Lionesses, the England team, higher level football. But when you go out on local parks, it's crap. It is. I've refereed a women's game before, and it was just awful. Absolutely appalling. It's a nice idea, and anyone who wants to should do what they want to do, that's fair enough. But they couldn't pass the ball, they were really clumsy. When you reach the higher level, they take it a bit more seriously, and then they're good.'
Alison Chapman,

'The first game I refereed was an under-17s game at Bracknell. I was nearly 15. All these guys were older than me, and at that age, 16, 17, they've got a lot to prove to their mates, so I got plenty of stick. I gave a penalty, and it was outside the box, but I couldn't back down. It was horrible, absolutely horrible.

'It's not so bad now. Most of the problems used to be with parents and girlfriends – I had a lot of trouble with girlfriends. I used to get called names, but I've always had a tough skin. In the first season, I took a lot of it to heart – you don't really know what to say when people start telling you how bad you are. There was a period when I thought, I can't carry on with this any more, but I was talked round. After my first season I'd got an answer for anything they had to say to me. It's water off a duck's back now. It goes right over my head, I really don't care any more.

'My very worst game was, without a doubt, in my first season up at Wycombe Park – two youth teams under-17, and absolutely everything went wrong. It was completely out of my control. Every decision I made someone contested it. During the game I saw one of the players was wearing one of those big sovereign rings so I said to him, "Take it off." So he says, "Look after it, stick it in your pocket."

'Later on in the game, one of the guys fouled somebody who had gone down on the ground and as he was going to get up, the other guy just booted him in the mouth. He'd got a mouthful of blood, teeth falling out everywhere, his Nan had come on to the pitch and she was whacking this bloke with her umbrella, and I was trying to send him off, trying to calm her down, trying to get the guy who was injured sorted out. It was just horrendous. It was one of those times when you think, this is never going to end.

'So it finally ended, and the guy with the ring came up, and said, "Can I have my ring back?" and I hadn't got it, so I said, "It's got to be

10 On the sidelines

Workers behind the scenes

The football on the pitch is only the tip of the iceberg. Behind the scenes is the vast infrastructure which keeps the sport going. Here are a few of the backroom heroes – the administrators, the referees, the people who look after the pitch, wash the kit and run the club shop, and the journalists whose careers are spent writing about the game they love.

THE ADMINISTRATOR
Reginald 'Chippy' Taylor

Reginald 'Chippy' Taylor

Whenever people reminisce about local football, it is not long before the name of Reginald 'Chippy' Taylor crops up. During his long involvement in the Sunday League and Berks and Bucks FA, Chippy became one of the most influential figures in the game. A former police officer who later worked for Berkshire County Council, Chippy was regarded as one of the best administrators in local football. He was a legendary character, a great debator with an encyclopaedic knowledge of football.

His long career as a football administrator began in 1952 when he took over as secretary of Tilehurst FC, which was on the point of folding. Over the years he built it up into a formidable side, but it was when he took over as General Secretary of the Reading and District Sunday League in 1969 that he really hit his stride.

The Sunday League officially started in 1964, with Brian Fielding as founding General Secretary. Roy Murdoch, chairman of the Reading Sunday League, takes up the story.

'In 1967-68, Brian Fielding was running the Torpedo side and he was talking about taking a touring team to Australia. The Sunday League was growing, pressures were building up and it was decided that Brian should stand aside as general secretary. The man who came in and took over the job was Chippy Taylor. Now Chippy was a real old Saturday man, a dry old stick, who had been in the Royal Berkshire Regiment and in the police force, but he came and took over.

'Looking back on the Sunday League, I'm very pleased we had a founding father like Brian Fielding who got the league going, but the time was right then to have a steady hand on the tiller and Chippy did a wonderful job. The beautiful thing about Chippy was that, although he'd very often go off and do his own thing, he would always bounce ideas off other people. Then he would say, 'This is what I think the best way of doing it is.' In his way he was a great democrat, but he did it in his own individual way.

'His great right hand was the original chairman of the league, Gordon Bartlett, who is now the president of the competition. Gordon went all the way along the line with Chippy. Arthur Scott, who had run Heron, became the deputy chairman, and I became chairman of the Youth League, which was developing into a very big league. Chippy told me that he wanted to have continuity, with age gaps between people so that, whatever happened, people who loved and appreciated the league would be there to follow through. Being an ex-soldier and an ex-policeman, he believed very firmly in the hierarchy principle of business management. That's what kept Chippy going.'

During that period Chippy was also deeply involved in the Youth League. Roy Budd, secretary of the Cavaliers (previously called Herons), has reason to be grateful to him.

'Chippy Taylor started the youth league. To be a club secretary you've got to have a terrific amount of dedication and to be a league secretary you need even more with all those teams and fixtures to look after. It was his brainwave to get a youth league. But there you are, he was a copper. He could see what was going on. There had been a complete change in the 1960s. National service had ended, and he must have felt there was a need. I suppose he put two and two together and thought a youth league would do a good job because it provided discipline. I've always thanked Chippy for starting it.'

Chippy continued to support the youth teams and helped Herons move up into the senior league, even though they had no permanent pitch – a constant problem in the town. Thanks to him they eventually made their base at Kings Meadow and then Coley rec, where they have played ever since. 'Old Chippy always kept his word,' said Roy.

Chippy revolutionised the Sunday League, building it up to become one of the best-run leagues in the south, so it was no surprise when the Berks and Bucks FA sought him out in 1980 as referees' secretary. Typically Chippy had already been grooming his replacement as general secretary, although this was news to the replacement. Norrie Hart was the Sunday League referees' secretary and he had no idea what Chippy was planning:

'The phone goes. It's Chippy Taylor.

' "Norrie," he said, "see you at my house in 10 minutes. I want to talk to you."

130

£75 or £85, and the referee gets £170. There's a big jump. Then the Premier League the referee gets £300, and so on. All linesmen are referees. There's a pyramid system. You'll referee at one level of the pyramid, and you're a linesman at the next.'

John: 'Unless you're a referee, you can't have a clue what refereeing is about. I think you've got to be in the club to understand. You ask any professional footballer, "Would you be a referee?" And they'd say, "Not a chance". They see it as this horrible profession that can't be any fun. And yet you talk to us and you'll find that we live and breathe football refereeing, and we love every second of it, even the bad moments. It's the same as being a copper. They have a hard time, but they have so much fun as well. They must do or they wouldn't do it.'

Norrie Hart

Norrie Hart, county official, former Referee of the Year, and now assessor of other referees, started refereeing in the 1950s in Scotland when he was doing his National Service, and was awarded his Class One by the RAF Football Association. 'I was never going to be the world's greatest footballer but I was an official of football with the black uniform and my Scottish FA badge. I was respected. In those days referees were respected. They called us Sir – it was expected of them.'

Things were different when he returned to in Reading and he did not referee officially again for 15 years.

'I shall never know how good I could have been if I hadn't had all those years out of the game and I envy those who have got the opportunity. But I packed it in to go back playing, and because I had a girlfriend that I was going to marry (but didn't).

'I had to start at the bottom as a Class Three again. The rules and everything about the game had changed. They didn't call you Sir any more unless it was spelt CUR. It was a very torrid start. I did quite well when I got back to the local level again. I did the Metropolitan League, some Southern League games, Isthmian League – the middle order.

'I learned an awful lot from a bloke called Ron Challis, who became a football league referee. The first time I saw him refereeing he said, "Anything you notice in particular?" So I said, "Yes, you've been giving lots of free kicks all over the park, sticking your hand up and having a word with people. Tell us what you're doing."

'He said, "That's called Challis's rule 12a. Anybody that upsets me, says anything, does anything, I carry the ball down to where he is, put the ball down, give him a direct free kick and if he says, "You can't do that, ref," I say, "Would you rather have a caution instead?"

'When I started as a referee in the services my first sending off was in an RAF v Navy inter-league game and I sent off a squadron leader. I must have been the most unpopular person on my station in Kinloss. I was too frightened to write, my hand was shaking so.'

Norrie Hart

137

'And I thought, I don't know about Challis's rule 12a, it's now Hart's rule 12a and I applied it. It means you don't have to bring your book out and caution them all the time because you don't book a player. Travel agents book, referees caution.

' I'm 65 years old and I'm terribly out of condition but as you get older you learn certain things about refereeing. One is to go wide. Instead of trying to go on your diagonal, which is something in the order of about 170 to 180 yards, you just drift wide towards the touch line. My eyes at a distance are good, close up they're diabolical. The number of times players have said to me, "Get your eyes tested, ref", and they were absolutely right. But I actually can see across the park going wide at an angle, and you don't have to run very fast.

'Another thing I've learned are the two rules of refereeing: Rule 1, the referee is always right; Rule 2 ,when the referee is wrong Rule 1 applies. Something players should always remember!'

THE PRESS
Biscuitmen and sausage rolls
by Maurice O'Brien, Reading News Agency

The sixth game of the 1995-96 season at Elm Park was a dreary affair – one of Reading's worst performances in recent memo-ry, illuminated only briefly by two examples of the impudent skills of James Lambert. It should have been something spe-cial, a spectacular display of footballing pyrotechnics studded with brilliant goals and outrageous moments of virtuosity, a match to remember.

But had I realised in advance that Port Vale's visit was the 600th consecutive senior Royals game I'd reported from the Elm Park press box I'd have anticipated that its quality would be depressingly similar to so many of the preceding 599.

Sure there was May 1995 and the First Division play-offs, the Division Two title win in such thrilling style 12 months earlier, the Simod Cup run, the 'Record Breaking Royals' of 85-86, a Fourth Division title in 1979 and a couple of phoenix-style pro-motions from the ashes of the Football League's basement.

And I've possibly broken the odd record myself down the years when you consider that I've written an average of 1,000 words on each one of those games – not counting the number of words spoken in scores of radio reports and commentaries.

But for all the good times there have also been many hours of spectacular under-achievement by a succession of Reading teams since the day in the late summer of 1973 when I strolled into Elm Park to report, for the first time, on the exploits of a team still somewhat quaintly known as The Biscuitmen.

And little did I realise the significance of the moment when Doris, a gutsy little lady whose kind heart and absolute loyalty was sadly to be cast aside as the seasons passed, took my first ever halftime order for tea and a sausage roll. It was waitress service if a newspaper or radio station required one's efforts during the interval but woe betide any reporter of an idle disposition who induced Doris to juggle her tray up the stairs under false pretences.

In those pre-executive box days the press accommodation was located at the back of the stand, a long, narrow construction with two rows of seats running the entire length of the box and catering at full capacity, which wasn't too often, for around 48 assorted hacks.

And curiously, at a time when Elm Park was almost the archetypal footballing backwater, it was one of the few press boxes in the land which was both enclosed AND had a heater. On cold days the windows steamed up horribly but the repeated use of a hanky to keep one's vision clear was a small price to pay for avoiding frost bite.

For some years the glass in front of my vantage point bore the imprint of a ball wildly misplaced by one of Percy Freeman's mulelike shots, or was it a pass? If the press box could withstand such an impact we decided that, in the event of war, we would adjourn there for the duration of hostilities.

But that sense of security proved sadly misplaced on April 24, 1976, when, thanks to goals from Robin Friday, Eamonn Dunphy and Dennis Nelson, Crewe Alexandra were vanquished 3-1 to ensure a third place finish in Division Four and take Reading back towards the promised land.

As we tried to share this momentous event with the outside world the more excitable elements of a 12,000 crowd were seeking the best position from which to salute 'Charlie Hurley's blue and white army'. First there was the rumbling of footsteps from above, next a snow shower of Polystyrene flakes from the ceiling and then... make no mistake it's extremely distracting trying to file 350 words to the *Sunday Express* with a large Doc Marten boot dangling inches from one's nose.

Incidentally I was sitting in that same seat after a home defeat by Bury only 10 months later when I phoned the larger-than-life Hurley at home to ask why he'd missed the post-match press conference only to be told in that deep baritone

'And curiously, at a time when Elm Park was almost the archetypal footballing backwater, it was one of the few press boxes in the land which was both enclosed AND had a heater. '

Maurice O'Brien

139

Former manager Maurice Evans – 'a true gentleman'

voice that he'd quit his job – at halftime!

Charlie was succeeded by Maurice Evans, a true gentleman possessing in abundance all the qualities sadly lacking from so many aspects of the game today. The familiar twinkle in his eye conveyed so much wisdom and good sense and yet ultimately wasn't enough to save him from the most heartless of sackings when Reading again stood third in the table and poised for elevation from the Fourth Division.

Brusque coach Ian Branfoot was already in position to take over and, despite a Third Division title and victory in the Simod Cup, should therefore hardly have been surprised at the timing and manner of his going when the moment came for the trapdoor to open beneath him.

Neither Branfoot nor successor Ian Porterfield were easy men for reporters to work with, a criticism which couldn't be levelled at Mark McGhee, who knew exactly what he wanted and the exciting fashion in which he was going to get it.

Sadly, because of the way his Royals love affair ended, some have seen fit to belittle McGhee's Elm Park efforts. With hindsight he would surely have stage managed his farewell a little better, but he was certainly a hard act to follow.

To their credit Mick Gooding and Jimmy Quinn managed it with a trip to Wembley and, at the time of writing, are still blazing new trails and proving a joy to quote-hungry reporters wearied by years of hackneyed managerial thoughts.

Like all Reading followers the press corps is caught in the limbo created by proposals for a move to a new ground. Our unique two-class society sees one contingent exposed, willingly or otherwise, to the elements while the less hardy members bask in the luxury of central heating and blue carpets.

But while the eyes of visiting scribes light up at such comfort, they find themselves in a false paradise. Because when the name Doris passed into the mists of time in press box legend – along with newsworthy characters like Mick Hollis, Gary Goodchild, Martyn Britten and Hughie Cheetham – so did those sausage rolls!

Not such a doddle
Steve Thomson, Reading Evening Post reporter 1983-89
Most people think covering a football club for the local paper must be a doddle – like having your hobby for a full-time occupation. But it can, in fact, be quite stressful at times – especially if you insist on sticking to the facts.

Even the invariably mild-mannered Maurice Evans once

11 Throw-ins and offsides
Anecdotes, stories and memories

NO MATCH FOR THE ROYALS
by David Barr

In the 1930s cinema-going was a way of life. The stars were household names. An English actress, Margaret Lockwood, would have rated highly – a demure Julia Roberts. When I won her in a competition organised by a magazine called Picturegoer, I was, as a randy 20-year-old, excited to say the least – and envied all round. I should add that I did not win her but a lunch with her. Not bad, I thought – and one never knew...

Margaret Lockwood (Hilton Tims collection)

The event was fixed for a Saturday (not as I would have planned it) and I duly turned up at Gainsborough Studios, Elstree (not all that far from Reading) at 11.30. It was 12 before it was realised that Margaret had got her lines crossed and was waiting hopefully at her flat at Dolphin Square in London. I, and the other winners, were rushed into a stretch limo (1936 version) to our lunch date. What I had planned was to get to Reading from Elstree in time for a 2.30 kick-off, F.A. Cup, Round Two, against mighty Wrexham from the Northern Section but it was one o'clock before I met Margaret.

I can't think why but I got the impression that she was not all that keen on her treat – formal too. It was not Margaret and Dave, but Miss Lockwood and Mr Barr. I hung around for another five minutes (no sign of food) and then said to myself, To hell with it.'You'll have to excuse me, Miss Lockwood' (she was probably Mrs Someonelse) 'but I have an important engagement in Berkshire.' With that I slipped off and got there in time to see Tommy Tait's first goal. A lot of my friends thought that I had gone mad.

A FOOTBALL TRAGEDY
by Bob Russell

My grandparents came to Reading from Wiltshire some time towards the end of the last century. At first they lived in Alpine Street, but later moved to a house in Orts Road, one of a number built by Huntley and Palmer for their employees. Grandfather was employed as a labourer and performed a number of duties during his employment. The family was large by modern standards, five daughters and three sons, of whom my father was the youngest, born in 1890. All the sons were educated at St John's School where the head was the never-to-be-forgotten Mr Bill Sadler, who saw little distinction between teaching and the administration of corporal punishment. Football was played at school and great store was placed on being good enough for a local amateur team. My father played for a team know as Clarence FC, but whom they played against or how good they were I have no knowledge.

Brigade Old Boys' Football Club 1907-8 –
Joseph Russell in back row, extreme left

Both my father, William, and his brother, Joseph, were members of the Boys Brigade, associated with St John's Church, in Watlington Street. Joseph played for the Brigade Old Boys FC 1907-8. In November of the following year, Joe suffered a fatal accident during a game. He was struck on the head and never recovered. He was buried on December 3 at Reading Cemetery. It must have been a traumatic and solemn Christmas for the family that year, and recalled each year at the festive season.

Football was not played again in the family and no further interest was ever taken.

GET ME TO THE MATCH ON TIME
by Peter Smith, former vicar of Bisham

A few years ago a Derbyshire vicar got himself some unwelcome publicity by apparently refusing to marry people on a Saturday afternoon if it stopped him watching Derby County's home games at the Baseball Ground. He had my sympathy because, although I have dissuaded a few couples from marrying on inconvenient dates which clashed with Reading's home games, I have never refused and, in fact, have missed one or two matches on account of weddings.

During my eight years as Vicar of Bisham, where Reading FC were regular visitors – to the Abbey not the church! – during the eighties for training sessions and youth team home games, I had one clash of interest which led to some dangerous driving between Bisham and Reading one Saturday in 1987.

I was approached some months before by two young hopefuls asking to be wed at Bisham on January 10 and saying that if I could not manage the day, they knew another clergyman not far away who would be only too pleased to tie the knot for them. Knowing the date to be the FA Cup Third Round day, I agreed to let the 'other chap' do the necessary (just in case Reading had a home draw). He agreed, and all seemed well, especially when the draw was made and included Reading v Arsenal for January 10, an all-ticket match. The other match at Bisham Church was timed for 2pm, an hour before kick-off at Elm Park, but having bought my tickets, I took the precaution of telephoning my intended deputy for the wedding. He had changed his mind and, far from being 'only too pleased' to come, he was going to be very busy and unable to spare the time!

Wedding ceremonies do not need to be prolonged; it is brides who insist on being late, and fussing photographers who prolong the occasions, not to mention the geography of some churches which can leave the Vicar trapped inside while the wedding guests are jamming the doorway trying to get out or take their own pictures.

January 10 was a very cold day but the bride's father wore a kilt (being a Scot). I managed to leave the wedding party on the river bank at Bisham while I ran to my waiting car at the church gate. Time? Around 2.30 and a mad dash ahead in a clapped-out old car through Sonning, Caversham, etc. At least I was able to drive up to the Wantage Road turnstiles, and leave my wife to navigate her own way out of Reading to do the shopping – a cruel thing on my part and she got lost.

So did we! By the time I worked my way into a spot where I could actually see the action, we were 1-2 down, and I had even missed Trevor Senior's goal. Of course Arsenal scored another goal to complete our misery, but it was worth the hassle.

Incidentally I never did discover what that other Vicar was doing that day – maybe he was watching Wycome Wanderers.

THE SAMARITANS
by David Downs

I was on holiday in Jersey in April, 1986, and Reading were playing away to Wolverhampton Wanderers in a vital Division Three fixture. I watched BBC TV News to see if the result would be given, but no luck. I rang a couple of pals back in Reading but they were out. I rang Jersey Radio and the Jersey Evening Post to see if they had the full-time results, but drew a blank.

By now I was getting desperate to find the result, and had almost given up hope when I saw a notice in the hotel phone booth, saying 'if worried, or in despair, ring the Samaritans', followed by a telephone number. I dialled the number and a very pleasant lady answered, 'Samaritans, can I help you?' The subsequent conversation went like this:

Anxious Reading FC supporter: 'I know this is an unusual request but do you have tonight's football results, please?'

Pleasant Samaritan Lady (giggling): 'No, I'm afraid we don't.'

ARFCS: 'It is rather important, it's Reading away to Wolves.'

PSL (stifling a laugh): 'Just a minute and I'll ask round the office.' (Long pause, punctuated by further suppressed giggles.) 'No, I'm afraid we don't have anyone here who knows the score.'

ARFCS: 'Oh dear, I thought you might be able to help.'

PSL: 'I'm sorry. You won't do anything silly, will you?'

ARFCS: 'No.'

I eventually found out the result (Reading had won 3-2) and when I returned to Reading after the holiday, sent the Jersey branch of the Samaritans a cheque of £5, just to prove that I hadn't topped myself simply because they couldn't let me know the result. I suggested that the Samaritans might use the fiver to employ someone to take down football scores each evening, and keep an up-to date-league table – just in case anyone in similar distress should call them.

HOW IT WAS THE DAY WE GOT PROMOTED FROM DIVISION FOUR
by M C Naptalie

I had been to a few games at Reading Football Club. This was the big one, the last game of the season with a television crew, the full works, as Reading were going to be promoted. To be part of the crowd, the joys, that feel-good feeling in the ground, the smiles, the songs, 'We are the South Bank boot boys, we are the South Bank boot boys'. It just takes you over. We all were at one for those 90 minutes. A team on and off the field. 'The ref needs glasses, the ref needs glasses', and we all sing as one in harmony.

For a young 15-year-old West Indian, being surrounded and out-numbered by male whites was quite a drastic move. But I love the game and was proud that my home town was moving up finally. We sang and I felt part of that oneness you get from being in a large group, even though I was there alone. It was a good game. I can't remember now if we won or not, just hearing the final whistle and rushing past the stewards to get on the pitch with everyone else, running across the pitch to greet and celebrate with the players. We sang, we clapped – real joyful feelings. Feeling good, Reading were up at last.

I left the ground with the crowd and was walking down the Oxford Road with hundreds of people. Then the celebrations suddenly and for no reason changed.

This police van pulled up by the side of me as we were walking. Out jumped this policeman, grabbed me by the arms and pushed me in the van. I resisted and asked what for. He said I had been seen stealing from off the pitch at Elm Park – one of the numbers from the hoardings. But I had no number, I was just enjoying myself.

There were a few other people in the van and I was getting frightened. What would mum say? I had never been in trouble, I was not a bad boy nor a trouble maker. Then the policeman who had pushed me in the van said to one of his mates, as he smashed his watch on the van, 'I'll claim that along with the overtime, I need a new watch'. He broke it when he was struggling with me.

It was a funny feeling. Such a nice day and here I was in a police van going down the cell for doing nothing but going to a game.What would mum say? She had a bad heart. Would she believe that I had done nothing wrong? I went to the cell, gave my address and telephone number. They went to contact my mum as I was under-age.

She came to my rescue, 110 per cent on my side, after she asked me the one question, 'Did you do it?' 'No, no, I did nothing, he just picked on me, mum.' She fought them all the way and in the end there was no charge. It was dropped because there was no evidence.

That day we got promoted from Division Four will always be with me. Not for the joy or the feeling, but how one man just like a ref (but in this case a policeman) can change the course of the day – the day we got promoted from Division Four.

I didn't go to the games for a while after that, but he didn't stop me from loving football or wanting to see it live.

MEMORABLE PLAYERS
Wooden legs, prima donnas and gigglers – a collection of characters from local football

❐ Phil Sarney of Caversham Athletic was a great character. Apparently he used to clutch a handkerchief while playing and you used to know when Phil was getting rattled when he started wiping at his brow and lips with his old rag. But there was one day that Wilf Fewtrell remembers seeing him, quite literally, losing his rag, when in a fit of anger, he threw it to the floor and protested to the referee, 'My ability, ref, they're destroying my ability. Tell 'em to go round me – not hit me!'
Duncan Mitchell

❐ We were playing a Berks and Bucks Senior match at Marlow Town's ground and on the coach going out, Bobby Parkes, who was a keen gambler, was saying to the lads, 'I've had a bet, I put a Yankee on today.' In the dressing room it was usual to hand over your watch and rings and money, put them in a bag and give them to somebody to keep on the line. Bob handed in his betting slip. He said, 'Don't lose it!' and all through the game he was shouting to the touch line, 'What won the 3.30?'
Peter Bartlett, West Reading

❐ February 1957: There was panic in the Lower Tilehurst dressing room just before the Berks and Bucks Cup tie against Blewbury. Star forward Ron Shepherd was missing, but he turned up seconds before the kick-off and breathlessly announced he had got married an hour earlier. All the excitement failed to affect his game and he scored a goal in the 12-2 thrashing of the North Berks visitors.

Nigel Sutcliffe, Reading Evening Post

❏ Ronny Eales of West Reading was a tremendous player. Once we were going by coach to a match and we had to pick up Ron at one o'clock. We stopped in the Oxford Road, Ron ran up, opened the coach door and said, 'Can you hold the coach for five minutes, the wife's just had a baby.' Incidentally, this baby was David who plays alongside my son Chris at Reading Town!

We used to play at the Mansion House and half an hour before kick-off we suddenly heard this awful noise. We looked outside and saw that Ron Eales, who was a scruffy, lovely, couldn't-care-less lad, had ridden his bike up all the way up from West Reading to the Mansion with no tyres on his bike. He just had the rims and we could hear this awful clanking.

We also had this centre forward called Tony Perrin who was a bank manager and he and Ron Eales met at Twyford station one morning. Ron was repairing a roof and was covered in black tar from head to foot. Tony Perrin was in his bowler hat with a rolled umbrella and people couldn't believe that these two were talking enthusiastically about the game on Saturday.

Jack Jarvis

❏ September 1908: Reading Reserves crushed Maidenhead Norfolkians 9-1 in a Great Western League game at Elm Park. Norfolkians' keeper 'Peggy' Gyngell gave a fine display and used his wooden leg to deflect shots round the post and over the bar.

Nigel Sutcliffe, Reading Evening Post·

❒ Three Mile Cross had a very very good player called Arthur Clifford. Off the pitch he was a hell of a gregarious fellow, cracking jokes, laughing, giggling. He only stood about 5 ft 7in, but built like a tank. If anything happened in that box, it would be perhaps five or six defenders in there with Arthur and one other Three Mile Cross player. When Arthur hit that box, everyone looked as though a bomb had hit them; the ball was in the net, and there was Arthur giggling and laughing. In the course of getting there, he'd probably thumped, barged, hurt or banged three or four players who were all holding different areas, and then afterwards he would be just grinning and laughing at you – no one could ever take umbrage at Arthur.

If you heard any laughing, a booming giggle coming from a dressing room that would be Arthur. What a character that man was, and he is still to this day. Everyone who goes down to the whippet racing or the dog racing will know him.

Roy Murdoch

❒ This West Reading player, who shall remain nameless, played on the Saturday, he played on the Sunday, he played on the Monday. We arranged a game on a Monday night, and he took off his jeans and his legs were absolutely covered in mud. He hadn't washed since Saturday.

Tony Bampton, West Reading

❒ Reading FC had a well-known goalkeeper in the 20s called Joe Duckworth. He had a very good – or a bad habit – of diving at centre-forwards' feet when they were just about ready to shoot at his goal. He'd make a headlong dive right at their feet – how he used to manage it I don't know. He used to catch it sometimes, in the head. But he saved hundreds of goals.

Richard Johnson

❒ When I made my debut at outside right as a raw 15-year-old for Reading GPO against the Reading Police, in a Wednesday League match in 1955, my opposite number at left back was none other than Bill Amor! Bill had played outside left for Reading FC's first team, from 1947 to 1951, England Amateurs, and was a member of the Great Britain Olympic Games football team of 1948. I recall I didn't get much of the ball in that match against Reading Police, and when I did I passed it back quickly to one of my team mates. Having watched and admired Bill from the Elm Park terraces when I was a small boy, I felt it wasn't right that I should actually try and take the ball past one of my heroes. I probably didn't have the confidence to do it anyway! However, my biggest thrill came at the end of the game, as the final whistle blew, when Bill Amor came over to me, shook my hand and said, 'Well played, son.' Happy days.

Bryan Horsnell

❒ When the twins, Tony and Terry Bampton played for West Reading we got used to them but other clubs got them muddled up. The first time they played for us was with West Reading Reserves. It was Kidmore End away. Tony was inside left, Terry was inside right and the chap who was centre forward was Ron Shepherd and he couldn't tell one from the other. When one of them had the ball he'd say, 'Here Terry, here Tony, here George, here Harry.' Knowing Ron, he'd probably had three or four pints before the game.

Peter Bartlett

❒ You take Neil Webb who plays for England. When he was 14, some of our lads were keeping him out of the local side. When Neil got to 15, our lads were smoking, kissing women, drinking. Neil Webb was working and pounding the streets and built himself up, so Neil went one

way and our lads went another. Neil had parental control. His father, Dougie who was an ex-pro, and his mum, Joan, are nice people, and they obviously got hold of Neil and said to him, 'You want to be a pro, son, well, you've got to act like a pro.'
Roland Ford

❏ I remember Archie (Stuart Lovell) got a bit of stick when he was an apprentice. One of our jobs was to clean the mini-bus that transported us to and from training. After giving it a clean, it was not unusual for us to roll the bus down the hill and then start it up and give it a bit of wheel spin. It all happened on the premises behind the away end at Elm Park so nobody got in the way. However, when Archie tried it he inadvertently put the bus in reverse and backed it into a gate and an adjoining wall, damaging the back lights and causing a dent in the vehicle. Poor old Stuart went as white as a ghost and faced a roasting from the staff. He promised faithfully he'd pay for the damage and worked all summer in Sainsbury's in order to raise the money. At the start of the new season he felt relieved he had raised enough to cover the costs and told Ian Branfoot. But Ian said he shouldn't have bothered because the damage had already been repaired – so his efforts were all in vain!
Adrian Williams

MEMORABLE MATCHES
Umbrellas, snakes and sausages – a few football classics

❏ I used to play for a team called St Luke's. Once I actually pushbiked to Binfield – and it was six-and-a-half miles from home – in pouring rain. The first sponsors of football in the country were the fishmongers, Eighteen. They didn't spend any money but what you used to get with your fish was a carrier bag with a Charles Eighteen advert on it, a thick cardboard top and a string handle, and all your kit used to fit into there. In those days you had a shirt supplied by some of the more wealthy clubs but the rest of it you supplied yourself – your socks, your shorts, anything you needed including pads. I found the safest pads in the world were two copies of the 'Horse and Hound' magazine, one down each sock well tied on, because they were really big thick ones. Well, I'd gone out all the way to Binfield in the pouring rain with this thing over the handlebars and you can imagine I was a right mess. As I turned into the gate – and I was saturated – Bernie, who was the manager, said, 'Flax, you're playing today.' I hadn't played for seven weeks because there were only 11 and that was it. I said, 'Oh great,' grabbed my bag and I got the string handle and the heavy cardboard piece but the rest of it had disintegrated. My big chance was going. So I said, 'Dear oh dear' – I've never in my life used foul language but I came very close to it on that occasion – and I stood there thinking, what do I do? when through the gate comes the village constable, a big fella called Tommy, 6ft 6in, on an old push bike with a pannier at the front and in that pannier were my boots and all my gear. He found them up on the Binfield road by the Shoulder of Mutton where he'd probably been in for a pint, knowing Tommy. So I got into the side and played football.
Norrie Hart

❏ The Borough Police were very strong in the Wednesday League. Everybody was out to beat the police in more ways than one! But they were very good, and we had some happy times. I was talking to one of the chaps from Tilehurst Football Club about old times, how we used to kick one another to bits, shake hands and have a pint afterwards. I was a bit of a tearaway in those days, you know, bull in a china shop, used to hit everything that was in front of me. I've been chased by a woman with an umbrella more than once. Up at Marlow, a woman chased me with an umbrella and a handbag 'cause I used to charge the goalkeeper. They weren't namby pamby people like they are today. If they had the ball in their area, you'd smack 'em.

Danny Webb

❒ Transport was playing RAF White Waltham away. They had to win the game to win the league and so did we. We won 3-2 eventually but they had a penalty and our goalkeeper, M May, saved it. Matey went in and put the boot in and our centre forward's mother, Mrs Gradbourne, she was on the pitch hitting this bloke with her umbrella. So football violence started a long time ago – in the 50s!

Roy Budd

❒ Oh, yes – you used to get some fouls; and fouls in those days were fouls. As you know, nowadays they wear almost dancing slippers for boots; years ago it was a real boot, up to here, a leather one, and I suppose it weighed almost as much as a navvy's boot, studded of course; and when they brought their leg up and kicked a bloke or brought it down his shins it really marked him. No doubt about it, they were wicked. They were for protection, you see, when football first started in the 1800s; but they're very different now. There's no protection in the shoes. If they get a kick or a boot comes down on their ankle or leg they just have to put up with it, and it cripples them.

Richard Johnson

❒ In September 1975, the linesman at the Reading v Rochdale match fell and broke his wrist, and I was asked to act as linesman for most of the match. I had to do it in my ordinary clothes, wearing my best shoes, but I felt quite confident, and it seemed to go all right. Then, in a Reading v Torquay United match, the referee was delayed because of a car crash, and I had to start the game as a linesman, though this time the club gave me a tracksuit to wear. Both times I was paid half a guinea by the Football League and received a congratulatory letter from the league secretary, Alan Hardaker, I nearly completed the hat trick because Clive Thomas was refereeing a Reading game and was unwell. He asked me to stand by for him in the dugout, but he managed to complete the ninety minutes and I haven't been called on since. Nowadays, of course, there is a fourth official in attendance at every first-class game.

Alan Porton, Reading Chronicle Sports Editor

❒ When I was in my first year as referee, I was at Bracknell Town and it was a very tense affair, a very close game. I was being assessed by one of the ex-top referees in the country except I didn't know this at the time. The ball ended up in the net, but the Bracknell guy had actually punched the ball in. I gave a hand signal for a free kick, but my signal wasn't that obvious, so people didn't understand whether I'd given the goal or not. Of course the defender was bigger than me, he was 6ft 6in, and he came running up to me, and he said, 'Did you give that goal, referee?' So I said, 'No, it was hand ball. It's your free kick'. He said, 'Oh, you are a darling', and he got hold of my head, turned it, and planted a big kiss on it. I felt so stupid.

John Moore

❒ **Tony Bampton** We had one memorable game when we played in the Berks and Bucks Intermediate cup at Thatcham who were in a higher league than us. It coincided with a squall